# DATE DUE

| | | | |
|---|---|---|---|
| OC 18 '99 | | | |
| MR 9 06 | | | |
| | | | |
| | | | |
| | | | |
| | | | |
| | | | |
| | | | |
| | | | |
| | | | |
| | | | |
| | | | |
| | | | |
| | | | |
| | | | |
| | | | |
| | | | |

DEMCO 38-296

R

# The Middle Kingdom Emerges

# GREG MASTEL

*M.E. Sharpe*
Armonk, New York
London, England

Copyright © 1997 by M. E. Sharpe, Inc.

**Library of Congress Cataloging-in-Publication Data**

Mastel, Greg, 1963–
The rise of the Chinese economy : the middle kingdom emerges /
Greg Mastel
p. cm.
Includes bibliographical references and index.
ISBN 0-7656-0017-X (hardcover : alk. paper ). —
ISBN 0-7656-0018-8 (pbk. : alk. paper)
1. China—Economic conditions—1976– 2. China—Economic
policy—1976– 3. China—Economic integration. I. Title.
HC427.92.M435 1997
338.951—dc21
96-53292
CIP

Printed in the United States of America

The paper used in this publication meets the minimum requirements of
American National Standard for Information Sciences—
Permanence of Paper for Printed Library Materials,
ANSI Z 39.48-1984.

BM (c)  10   9   8   7   6   5   4   3   2   1
BM (p)  10   9   8   7   6   5   4   3   2   1

# Contents

# List of Tables and Figures

## Tables

# Acknowledgments

The author wishes to gratefully acknowledge the enormous assistance provided by Lois F. Hayes in all aspects of the preparation of this book, and of Andrew Z. Szamosszegi in the preparation of tables and graphs. In addition, the entire staff of the Economic Strategy Institute provided endless support and assistance throughout the writing process. The responsibility for any errors, however, rests solely with the author.

The
RISE of the
CHINESE
ECONOMY

# 1

# Introduction

In 1978, China embarked upon the greatest economic experiment in modern history. Deng Xiaoping launched a bold effort to reform China's economy and open economic ties with the noncommunist world. This effort involved injecting more market economics into China's moribund communist system and creating Special Economic Zones (SEZs) to stimulate trade with western countries.[1] These policies have created something akin to a modern-day gold rush, with western businesses investing heavily in China. Despite setbacks like Tiananmen Square, the look and culture of southern China has been fundamentally and probably irreversibly changed by these events.

Driven by the twin engines of foreign investment and exports, China has grown at a spectacular rate in recent years. Since 1990, China's growth has been in the double digits. This feat has been achieved while running a trade surplus, attracting a tremendous flow of foreign investment, and keeping inflation generally under control.[2] No other country has been able to simultaneously achieve all of these economic marks.

In addition to growing at a rapid pace, the level of development in China has also increased. Per capita income is still low, but Chinese industry has surged forward. In less than two decades, China has been transformed from a near stone age economy to a full-fledged industrial power. China has gone from having virtually no trade with the world to being one of the world's ten largest exporters.[3] Increasingly, its exports have become more sophisticated. Advanced export categories, such as

3

electronic products, have surged. Surprisingly, 80 percent of China's exports are manufactured products; the United States cannot match that figure.[4]

Most notably, if China is able to continue to keep foreign investment and exports high and, as a result, enjoy strong growth, it will become the world's largest economy early in the next century. This is not to suggest, however, that China's economy will be the equal of the world's big three economies—the United States, Japan, and the European Union—in all respects. For decades to come, China will face regional disparities and other development problems that the big three have overcome. Nonetheless, China is certain to become an ever more important player in the world economy.

Unfortunately, that is not necessarily good news. Although China has undertaken substantial economic reforms, it would be an overstatement to say that it has completely abandoned communism. The state still plays a major role in directing or, at least, controlling economic activity. The exchange rate of China's currency is set by the government. Though there have been substantial efforts at reform, state-owned enterprises (SOEs) still account for about one-third of China's gross domestic product (GDP). In addition, there is a large portion of the Chinese economy linked to an ill-defined category of enterprises referred to as collectives. These collectives are a diverse group ranging from subsidiaries of SOEs, enterprises owned by state and local governments, to ventures that might truly be thought of as private enterprises, but most are still closely tied to the government.[5]

The Chinese government's control of the economy stretches well beyond the enterprises it owns. Much of the machinery of communism is still alive and well. A new five-year economic plan was released early in 1996, government blueprints for "pillar" industries have long been in place, and new government industrial plans have been released for several industries.[6] The policies unveiled in these plans effect all enterprises operating in China—government and private, foreign and domestic.

Despite the economic reforms that have taken place, the expansive role of the government in setting economic policy seems likely to continue. Chinese leaders seem comfortable with an economy that attempts to merge some elements of communism with some elements of capitalism. Terms, like market-based socialism, are frequently used in Chinese visions of the economic future.

This mixed economic system has obviously worked well for China in recent years, but as China becomes a more important player in the world economy, its unique economic system will pose substantial problems..The recent discussion of this problem has focused upon attempts to integrate China into existing global economic institutions, such as the World Trade Organization (WTO) and the Group of Seven (G-7).

China has focused most of its attention upon gaining membership in the WTO to ensure that its export growth can continue. Historically, however, the WTO was conceived as an organization of free-trade market economies to serve as an economic counterpart to the communist system. How, then, is it possible to incorporate a country that still maintains so much state control of its economy along with many trade barriers into an organization aimed at free trade? No adequate answer has yet been formulated to this simple question.

China's membership in the G-7 seems equally problematic. The G-7 is an organization of the world's largest free-market democracies. Since China is neither a free market nor a democracy, its credentials for membership are immediately in doubt.

Nonetheless, as China's economy grows, pressure increases to integrate China into the existing global economic institutions or at least to find a way for these institutions to deal with the new economic power. This task is probably the most important economic challenge on the horizon for the world economy. Further, as if China was not enough of a challenge, the precedents set in dealing with China will shape the policy for dealing with many similarly situated countries, like Russia and Vietnam, who also seek entry to these global institutions.

To shed some light on China's integration into the global community, this book attempts to address three topics. First, it makes a detailed analysis of the Chinese economy and Chinese economic policy. Second, it analyzes the problems that must be confronted to integrate China into the world economy. Third, it suggests some possible approaches to solving those problems. Hopefully, the discussion will shed some light on the critical policy questions raised by China's emergence as an economic superpower.

## Notes

1. H. Jacobson and M. Oksenberg, *China's Participation in the IMF, the World Bank, and the GATT: Toward a Global Economic Order* (Ann Arbor: University of Michigan Press, 1990).

2. World Bank, *The Chinese Economy: Fighting Inflation, Deepening Reforms, a World Bank Country Study* (Washington, DC: The World Bank, 1996).

3. Statement based upon IMF world trade statistics for 1996.

4. Ministry of Foreign Economic Relations and Trade, *Almanac of China's Foreign Economic Relations and Trade,* 1993, 479; Department of Commerce statistics.

5. World Bank, *Bureaucrats in Business* (Oxford: Oxford University Press, 1995), 66.

6. United States Trade Representative, *1996 National Trade Estimate Report on Foreign Trade Barriers* (Washington, DC: USTR, 1996), 46.

# Part I

## China's Political and Economic World

# 2

# The Chinese Economy

Since China began its great economic experiment in the late 1970s, its economy has grown at a spectacular pace. Over the past fifteen years, the Chinese economy has grown at a nearly double-digit rate. From 1989 to 1991, China experienced a brief growth slowdown during which the economy grew at only about 5.4 percent—about two and a half times the U.S. growth rate for the last decade. Since this slowdown, China's annual growth rebounded solidly to double-digit rates.[1] In 1995 and 1996, China instituted some restrictive economic policies to dampen inflation and began to experience an economic slowdown. In spite of these developments, growth for 1996 held at over 9 percent.[2]

Though these statistics may sound impressive, they simply do not do justice to this enormous economic achievement. Even though China surely still has economic problems, such as regional disparities, inflation, and low average incomes, China's growth over the last two decades is probably the greatest economic achievement of the later half of the twentieth century. Though its long-term implications are still unclear, this growth surge ranks at least with the emergence of the United States as an economic power and the postwar recovery of Germany and Japan. Coastal China has been transformed from an agrarian economy into an industrial powerhouse.

This dramatic rise can be traced back to two powerful engines of growth: foreign investment and exports. Foreign investment has been a particularly important factor in China's growth in the

1990s, increasing at a nearly exponential rate. Total foreign investment contracts in 1992 and 1993 exceeded all contracted investment in China in previous years for which records are available.[3] China now ranks second only to the United States as a recipient of foreign investment.[4]

China's export growth has been even more impressive. Unlike other communist countries, China looked to western export markets since its break with the Soviet Union in the early 1960s. Its efforts at finding western export markets, however, bore fruit only after it began economic reforms.[5] Over the last two decades, China's exports have grown at three times the world average rate. From the mid-1980s to the mid-1990s, China's exports grew at nearly 20 percent annually.[6] This export success brought a steady stream of foreign hard currency into China and spurred enormous growth.

These sources of growth have built the China that now seeks to join the global trading system and other economic institutions; no longer a poor developing economic basket case, China is an emerging economic powerhouse built on many of the same policies as its East Asian neighbors, such as South Korea, Taiwan, and Japan, but with the resources to grow even larger. To appreciate the issues raised by China's effort to integrate itself into global economic institutions, it is necessary to understand more fully the current state and future prospects of the Chinese economy.

**The Numbers Game: Problems with Statistics**

A problem that emerges again and again in analyzing the Chinese economy is the lack of reliable economic statistics. With regard to China, there is wide debate over such relatively simple issues as the size of the Chinese economy and the size of the state-owned portion of the economy. Chinese official statistics on many issues ranging from exports to investment are sometimes questionable or unavailable,[7] but there is often no other reliable independent information. Estimates from other sources often rely upon Chinese data. On matters of potential political controversy, such as the size of China's trade balance, this poses a serious problem.

Outside economists have derived ingenious methods to estimate important statistics indirectly using more easily verifiable data. Unfortunately, as the authors often admit, these are not always entirely reliable. As fascinating as these debates are, however, they are not the core topic of this discussion. Thus, for the purpose of this book, every effort is made to employ the most credible third-party estimates on economic statistics. Most frequently, data are drawn from the World Bank, the International Monetary Fund (IMF), and, for some U.S.-China trade issues, the U.S. Commerce Department. Certainly, these data are also open to debate, but they comprise the best information available. Also, unless otherwise noted, the relatively small disputes over data make little difference as to ultimate policy recommendations, which are the primary topic of this book. Still, the reader should be aware of possible data deficiencies inherent in any discussion of this topic.

### The Size and Prospects for Growth of the Chinese Economy

One of the most serious debates over the data on the Chinese economy focuses upon the size of China's GNP. There is no clear consensus among economists who have attempted to estimate the size of China's economy using methods ranging from estimating the purchasing power of Chinese currency to examining the eating habits of Chinese citizens.[8] This has resulted in a significant range of estimates, which are listed in Table 2.1.

Credible recent estimates based on the yuan's purchasing power generally place the Chinese economy in the range of $2.0 to $3.2 trillion. The most recent estimate by the World Bank falls into this range,[9] which will be employed in other calculations used in this discussion. Of course, if estimates significantly outside this range are employed, a very different picture of the Chinese economy can be painted.

Table 2.1

**Estimates of China's GNP per Capita and GNP**

| | Year | GNP per capita (dollars) | GNP (billions of dollars) |
|---|---|---|---|
| Exchange rate based | | | |
| Garnaut & MA (1992) | 1987 | 850 | 939 |
| Perkins (1992) | 1990 | 1,000 | 1,153 |
| "China GNP per Capita," 1994 | 1991 | 442 | 517 |
| World Development Report, 1994 | 1992 | 470 | 556 |
| World Development Report, 1996 | 1994 | 530 | 631 |
| | | | |
| Purchasing power parity based | | | |
| Lardy (1993, 1994) | 1990 | 1,000–2,000 | 1,140–1,370 |
| Penn World Tables | 1990 | 2,700 | 3,114 |
| World Development Report— | | 2,200 | 2,574 |
| Regression | 1991 | | |
| World Development Report— | | 1,460 | 1,728 |
| Secondary prices | 1992 | | |
| "China GNP per Capita," 1994 | 1992 | below 2,000 | below 2,367 |

Source: Various issues, *World Bank Development Report,* "China's GNP per Capita."

If this range is accepted, it would make China the world's third largest national economy. It is considerably behind the U.S. economy, at $7 trillion the world's largest, but rapidly approaching that of Japan, which is now $4.3 trillion (see Figure 2.1). It would also mean that China's economy is already significantly larger than the national economy of Germany, but still smaller than that of the European Union, which is normally considered as a single economic unit.

China's growth rate far exceeds that of any of the world's other economic powers. China has been growing at a double-digit rate in the last four years, and there is good reason to expect this to continue. China's economic fundamentals appear promising. Although difficult to estimate with great certainty, saving and investment levels remain high.[10] China has a vast and well-educated work force that could support significant growth, partic-

Figure 2.1.  **China's Real GDP Growth Rate, 1980–1995**

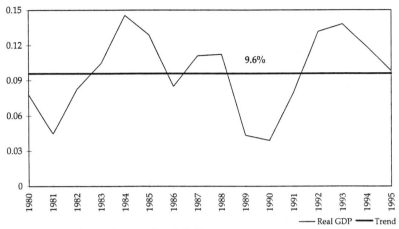

*Source:* International Monetary Fund (IMF).

ularly as new technologies are adopted. Industrialization seems to be moving slowly from the coastal provinces to interior provinces, which would open new resources for future economic growth.[11]

Some predict both food[12] and energy[13] shortfalls for China, but domestic production, particularly of food, has shown promising signs of growth. Further, thanks to continuing export earnings, foreign exchange reserves, and an almost limitless ability to borrow internationally at below-market rates, China seems well equipped to import needed supplies.

A political crisis, such as domestic revolution or civil war, would, of course, dramatically affect economic estimates. This topic is discussed in more detail in the next chapter, but suffice it to say that the prospect for a political upheaval that would affect growth seems unlikely in the short term. The continuing flow of investment indicates that investment markets have made a similar judgment.

As will be discussed in more detail in subsequent sections, both foreign investment and exports promise to spur continued economic growth. It will be nearly impossible, however, for the flow of outside investment to continue to increase at exponential

**Figure 2.2. Extrapolating U.S. and Chinese Growth Paths, 1994–2015**

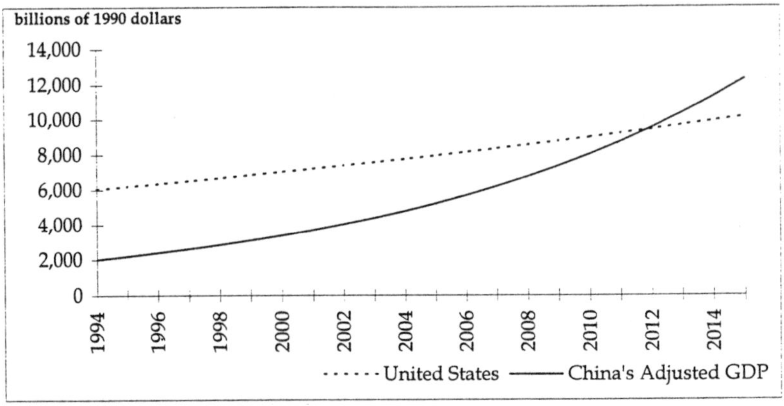

billions of 1990 dollars

14,000
12,000
10,000
8,000
6,000
4,000
2,000
0

1994 1996 1998 2000 2002 2004 2006 2008 2010 2012 2014

······ United States ——— China's Adjusted GDP

*Sources:* IMF; *The Economist,* "The Titan Stirs."
*Note:* The *Economist* estimate of China's 1991 GDP was adjusted by applying the IMF's real GDP growth rates for 1992–1994. For 1995–2015, a growth rate of 2.5 percent was assumed for the U.S. economy, and 9 percent growth rate was assumed for China. This follows the *Economist* estimate, which assumed China's growth rate would annually be 6.5 percent higher than the U.S. growth rate.

rates without draining world capital markets. Although there are indications that foreign investment growth is stabilizing and that China is becoming more restrictive in its treatment of foreign investment, investment seems likely to continue at present levels for some time. Further, as western companies build large manufacturing and operating bases in China, the ongoing maintenance and supply demands of these operations virtually guarantee a continuing flow of funds for the foreseeable future. Given the long-term perspectives of many of China's investors, and attempts by China to discourage an outward flow of funds, sustained significant outflows are unlikely into the next century.

Export prospects are also good. By most estimates, China is still less trade-dependent than other East Asian economies.[14] Even if China is not admitted to the WTO, most countries that are members automatically extend most of the benefits of WTO trade barrier cuts to China.[15] China has already established itself in the production of many "low-end" manufactured products.[16]

This strong comparative advantage will create new export opportunities. In addition, China is establishing itself as a producer of a wide range of other manufactured products. In short, export growth promises to support substantial additional Chinese growth.

The *Economist* magazine was the first to note in 1992 that if China's economy merely continued at a rate of 8 percent and other economies grew at their present rates, China would become the world's largest economy by 2010 (see Figure 2.2).[17] Many critics rightly noted that such a simple straight line extrapolation made many questionable assumptions.[18] It is certainly possible that economic events over the next fifteen years will throw this estimate off, perhaps by decades. In the years since the *Economist*'s estimate, however, China has actually grown faster than the rate the *Economist* assumed. Judging from current economic conditions, the estimate seems entirely reasonable. Further, even if estimates are off by a significant degree, China is still likely to become the world's largest economy within the lifetime of most readers.

**Foreign Direct Investment**

As mentioned, China has experienced a tremendous surge of foreign direct investment (FDI) in the 1990s (see Figure 2.3). FDI has surged to a level of nearly $40 billion per year, making China a leading target of FDI, second only to the United States. In 1995, China received six times as much investment as the second-place developing country recipient of FDI, Malaysia. In 1990, inward FDI was less than $4 billion but grew to $38 billion by 1995.[19] This ninefold increase is perhaps the most dramatic facet of the Chinese economic miracle. Here again, there are some uncertainties regarding data; exchange rates, the close links between China and Hong Kong, and reinvestment of profits in China all complicate data collection and interpretation.

The causes of the surge in FDI are many and varied. The most compelling feature of China as an investment site is the rapid

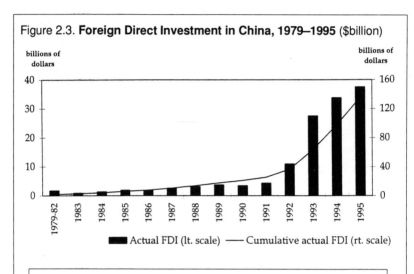

Figure 2.3. **Foreign Direct Investment in China, 1979–1995** ($billion)

|  | Actual FDI (lt. scale) | Cumulative actual FDI (rt. scale) |
|---|---|---|
| 1979–82 | 1.77 | 1.77 |
| 1983 | 0.92 | 2.69 |
| 1984 | 1.42 | 4.11 |
| 1985 | 1.96 | 6.06 |
| 1986 | 1.88 | 7.94 |
| 1987 | 2.65 | 10.58 |
| 1988 | 3.19 | 13.78 |
| 1989 | 3.77 | 17.55 |
| 1990 | 3.49 | 21.04 |
| 1991 | 4.37 | 25.41 |
| 1992 | 11.01 | 36.41 |
| 1993 | 27.52 | 63.93 |
| 1994 | 33.77 | 97.70 |
| 1995 | 37.52 | 135.22 |

*Source:* Ministry of Foreign Trade and Economic Cooperation.

growth of the Chinese economy and the enormous market that it promises to become in the future. For many firms, China, with its low-cost, high-skill work force, has also developed into an attractive site for assembly manufacturing. Components from other countries are often shipped to China for final assembly and later exported to other markets.[20] Seeing the economic development

Figure 2.4.  **Sources of FDI in China, 1995**

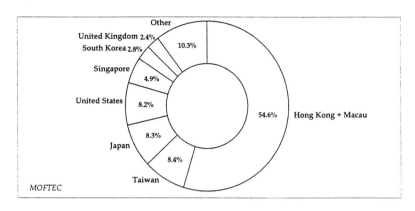

*Source:* Ministry of Foreign Trade and Economic Cooperation.

potential of this type of assembly operation, China has encouraged it and, through investment performance requirements, which are discussed in later chapters, virtually mandated it. China has also created a legal environment that is generally friendly to FDI, though recent changes in this regard raise some uncertainty for the future.

Most industrialized countries have taken part in the investment surge into China. The four leading sources of FDI into China are, in order, Hong Kong, Taiwan, Japan, and the United States (see Figure 2.4). The leading roles of Hong Kong and Taiwan are not surprising. China, Hong Kong, and Taiwan make up what is often referred to as Greater China and form, in some respects, a single economic unit. As of the summer of 1997, control of Hong Kong will actually revert to China, though China has promised to allow it to retain some independence.[21] Regardless of what happens in terms of political control, however, economic unification between Hong Kong and China has been a reality for some time. Hong Kong is essentially China's port to the world, and most economic activity in Hong Kong is directed at China.

Taiwan's status as a leading source of FDI is more surprising given the enmity between the governments of Taiwan and the mainland. The roots of Taiwan's current government can be traced back to the Chinese nationalists that fled the mainland after the communist revolution in 1949. For years, the government of Taiwan claimed to be China's government in exile.[22] Still, Taiwan's cultural and family ties to the mainland are very strong. Since China began to allow it, a significant amount of money has flowed from people in Taiwan to their relatives in mainland China.[23] Further, as wages have risen in Taiwan, it has become a less attractive site for low-end manufacturing. As the Chinese economy has opened, many Taiwanese businesses engaged in the manufacture of toys, apparel, and similar products have moved operations to the mainland.

Japan's role as a source of FDI also warrants some discussion. Until 1994 and for many years previously, the United States was the third largest source of FDI into China. Like most industrialized countries, Japan sought investment in China. Cultural tensions between Japan and China dating back to World War II and before, however, limited Japanese investment in China. Further, Japanese companies have traditionally strived to keep manufacturing facilities within Japan.[24] The rising value of the yen, however, has made it increasingly difficult for Japanese companies to manufacture in Japan;[25] China is a very attractive offshore manufacturing site.

Also, Japan has focused much of its overseas aid program upon China. Some of this aid is tied to, or must be spent to buy, Japanese products, and this obviously creates a foothold for Japanese companies. International pressure has forced Japan to untie most of its aid, but there are continuing questions as to the nature of Japanese aid.[26] During the same period, the United States has limited aid to China due to budget cuts and sanctions dating to the Tiananmen Square massacre.[27] This disparity in aid has also helped Japanese companies move ahead of the United States as a source of investment into China.

The United States remains, however, a major source of investment into China (see Table 2.2). Somewhat surprisingly, the larg-

Table 2.2

**Composition of U.S. Foreign Direct Investment in China, on a Historical-Cost Basis, 1995**

| Industry | Share of total FDI |
|---|---|
| All industries | 100.0% |
| Petroleum | 39.8% |
| Manufacturing | 45.0% |
|    Food and kindred products | 3.0% |
|    Chemicals and allied products | 8.7% |
|    Primary and fabricated materials | 1.0% |
|    Industrial machinery and equipment | 3.4% |
|    Electronic and transportation equipment | 23.3% |
|    Other manufacturing | 5.7% |
| Wholesale trade | 4.8% |
| Banking, finance, insurance, real estate, and services | 3.7% |
| Other industries | 6.8% |

*Source:* Bureau of Economic Analysis, U.S. Department of Commerce.

est U.S. investments in China are not in apparel or other low-end products, but in automobile and electronic manufacturing. Beijing Jeep is the oldest and one of the largest foreign-owned auto ventures in China.[28] The investments of Motorola in semiconductor and electronic manufacturing facilities have led the way for other U.S. electronics investments.[29] Still, there are substantial U.S. investments in low-end manufacturing. Competitive forces and the urging of the Chinese government will likely convince many U.S. firms in a variety of industries to continue some level of investment in China.

Overall, most FDI in China is still focused in low-end manufacturing. Many of these investments are simple assembly and re-export plants. Just as is the case with U.S. companies, however, companies from many developed economies have invested in more advanced manufacturing sectors, such as automobiles, electronics, and even aerospace. Some of these investments are doubtlessly aimed at currying favor from Beijing, with an eye toward winning large contracts, but the size and continuing nature of the investments indicate that China plays a larger role in many of these companies' business plans. Some U.S. service firms have also made substantial investments in China,[30] but in many service sectors, China imposes investment restrictions. It is worth noting that investment figures are another area where statistical discrepancies arise. The most common of these stems from sources mixing statistics on promised investment and actual investment.

What does the future hold for FDI flows into China? As noted previously, the growth of FDI in the early 1990s is almost certainly not sustainable, but a continued strong flow of FDI seems likely for two reasons. First, there are still sound fundamental reasons to invest in China. China provides a good labor pool, a promising developing market, and a springboard into other Asian markets. In some sectors, concerns such as the lack of protection of intellectual property in China have become significant enough to discourage further investment. On the whole, however, there appears to be considerable potential for growth of FDI in many sectors.

From a political perspective, China is also likely to remain an attractive site for FDI. As is discussed in more detail in the next chapter, investors seem little concerned with the prospects for political upheaval, and there is no evidence of a crisis looming in the short term. China's future policy on investment is a more open question.[31] As is discussed in great detail in forthcoming sections, China's new investment policies do indicate some reservations about foreign investment. On the whole, however, China is unlikely to intentionally "kill the goose that lays the golden eggs" by slamming the door on FDI.

## Foreign Trade

Given the focus of this book on China's efforts to join the WTO, an economic analysis of its trade performance is particularly relevant. As noted, China's export performance has been impressive. Chinese exports have grown at three times the world average rate over the last eighteen years. For much of that period, they grew

Table 2.3

**Exports and Imports of Goods and Services as a Share of GDP, 1994**

|  | Exports | Imports |
|---|---|---|
| China | 23.1% | 22.4% |
| Chile | 28.7% | 31.0% |
| Indonesia | 28.9% | 31.3% |
| Korea | 31.2% | 32.7% |
| Philippines | 36.0% | 42.3% |
| Thailand | 40.8% | 47.0% |
| Taiwan | 47.1% | 45.0% |
| Malaysia | 91.1% | 100.5% |

*Source: World Markets Executive Overview* (DRI/McGraw Hill, 1995).

at an incredible 25 percent per year; as a result, China was cata-pulted onto the list of the world's top ten exporters.[32] This is a feat that ranks China with other export powerhouses, notably Japan and South Korea. Although these statistics are open to some dispute because of uncertainty over the correct figure to employ for China's GDP, comparison with other economies would seem to indicate that China still has substantial potential to increase its export dependence (see Table 2.3).[33]

China's initial export success revolved around exporting low-end manufactured products to major developed markets. The United States, Japan, and the EU absorbed much of China's surging exports. As will be discussed in more detail below, China lists Hong Kong as its major export market, but much of those exports are ultimately destined for other markets. China has also had some success in exporting to a long list of other export markets (see Table 2.4). Most of this export success has been led by exports of low-end manufactures, such as apparel, toys, and games. China seems to possess a strong comparative advantage over the rest of the world in the production of these goods (see Table 2.5).

China has not followed the typical pattern of emerging econo-mies of first gaining a foothold by exporting agricultural or natu-ral resource products and then developing a manufacturing base.

Table 2.4

**China's Major Export Markets, as Reported by China, 1995**

|  | Exports | Share of total |
|---|---|---|
| Hong Kong | 36,003 | 24.2% |
| Japan | 28,466 | 19.1% |
| United States | 24,744 | 16.6% |
| Korea | 6,688 | 4.5% |
| Germany | 5,672 | 3.8% |
| Singapore | 3,500 | 2.4% |
| Netherlands | 3,233 | 2.2% |
| Taiwan | 3,095 | 2.1% |
| United Kingdom | 2,791 | 1.9% |
| Italy | 2,067 | 1.4% |
| France | 1,844 | 1.2% |
| Thailand | 1,752 | 1.2% |
| Russia | 1,674 | 1.1% |
| Australia | 1,626 | 1.1% |
| Indonesia | 1,438 | 1.0% |
| Canada | 1,362 | 0.9% |
| Malaysia | 1,281 | 0.9% |

*Source:* International Monetary Fund.

Already, more than 80 percent of China's exports are manufactured products.[34] Interestingly, that figure is somewhat higher than the level of manufactured exports from the United States. Further, China does not seem satisfied with simply exploiting its advantage in the manufacture of apparel. China has increased its export of electrical machinery and apparatus by 190 percent over the last three years.[35] Admittedly, the category may be so broad as to give a somewhat deceptive impression of China's export success. A closer examination of selected high-technology exports, however, confirms the increasing presence of China in the manufacture of high-tech products (see Table 2.6). For example, China now manufactures aerospace parts for all of the world's manufacturers of large commercial aircraft.[36]

China will also have increased opportunities to export its products. Obviously, if China's efforts to join the WTO succeed, it will have more secure access to export markets. But the WTO will benefit China even if it is not a member. Most countries

Table 2.5

**China's Top Twenty Exports, by 3-digit SITC Code, 1992–1995, sorted by 1995 totals** ($thousand)

| Rank | | SITC R.3 | 1992 | 1995 |
|---|---|---|---|---|
| 1 | Footwear | 851 | 4,242,135 | 6,661,730 |
| 2 | Men's, boys'clothing, x-knit | 841 | 4,600,237 | 6,321,634 |
| 3 | Women's, girls'clothing, x-knit | 842 | 4,644,562 | 5,971,981 |
| 4 | Other textile apparel | 845 | 4,034,750 | 5,966,900 |
| 5 | Baby carriages, toys, games | 894 | 3,483,047 | 5,922,811 |
| 6 | Telecom. equipment and parts | 764 | 1,350,368 | 4,044,012 |
| 7 | Cotton fabrics, woven | 652 | 2,057,215 | 3,411,107 |
| 8 | Misc. manufactured goods | 899 | 1,710,225 | 2,889,960 |
| 9 | Trunks, suitcases, bags, etc. | 831 | 1,476,635 | 2,869,573 |
| 10 | Clothing, nontextile; headgear | 848 | 1,539,155 | 2,766,393 |
| 11 | Textile articles | 658 | 1,703,570 | 2,563,762 |
| 12 | Radio-broadcast receiver | 762 | 1,484,204 | 2,555,296 |
| 13 | Articles, of plastic | 893 | 1,125,649 | 2,475,121 |
| 14 | Fabrics, man-made fibers | 653 | 1,346,978 | 2,470,070 |
| 15 | Electrical machinery and apparatus | 778 | 837,990 | 2,430,243 |
| 16 | Automatic data processing equipment | 752 | 301,086 | 2,301,505 |
| 17 | Petroleum oils, crude | 333 | 2,774,490 | 2,236,367 |
| 18 | Watches and clocks | 885 | 1,358,351 | 2,095,542 |
| 19 | Textile yarn | 651 | 1,344,101 | 2,095,354 |
| 20 | Pig iron, etc. | 671 | 413,983 | 1,779,602 |

*Source:* United Nations Comtrade Database.

extend most-favored-nation (MFN) trading status to China. This means that trade concessions granted as a result of the establishment of the WTO automatically include China. Thus, China's exports will benefit from WTO tariff cuts even if it is not a WTO member.[37] As the world's largest textile exporter, China in particular stands to benefit from the phase-out of current quotas on textiles and apparel, a step that could open significant new markets for textile exporters. In a recent bilateral understanding on textiles, China agreed to limits on textile exports to the U.S. market until 2005, notwithstanding China's possible entry into the WTO.[38] Even if it is not entirely freed from textile quotas, however, China will at least reap significant tariff benefits from the WTO.

Table 2.6

**Export Performance of High-Tech Items, 1992 and 1995** (thousand and percent)

| | SITC R. 3 | 1992 | 1995 | Growth |
|---|---|---|---|---|
| Telcom. equipment and parts | 764 | 1,350,368 | 4,044,012 | 199% |
| Radio-broadcast receiver | 762 | 1,484,204 | 2,555,296 | 72% |
| Electrical machinery and apparatus | 778 | 837,990 | 2,430,243 | 190% |
| Automatic data-processing equipment | 752 | 301,086 | 2,301,505 | 664% |
| Parts for office machines | 759 | 579,630 | 1,650,466 | 185% |
| Electronic switching and relay circuitry | 772 | 534,668 | 1,630,104 | 205% |
| Electric power machinery parts | 771 | 448,100 | 1,545,276 | 245% |
| Domestic electrical, non-elec. equip. | 775 | 704,977 | 1,391,410 | 97% |
| Transistors, valves, etc. | 776 | 310,543 | 1,294,618 | 317% |
| Rotating electric plant | 716 | 558,647 | 1,080,420 | 93% |
| Office machines | 751 | 252,072 | 850,747 | 238% |
| Electro-medical, x-ray equip. | 774 | 10,781 | 40,454 | 275% |
| | | | | |
| Memo: Total Exports | | 84,940,060 | 148,779,563 | 75% |

*Source:* United Nations Comtrade Database.

Table 2.7

**Leading Exporters and Importers of World Merchandise Trade, 1994**
($billion)

| Rank | Exporter | Value of exports | Rank | Importer | Value of imports |
|---|---|---|---|---|---|
| 1 | United States | 512.5 | 1 | United States | 689.2 |
| 2 | Germany | 424 | 2 | Germany | 378 |
| 3 | Japan | 397 | 3 | Japan | 275.2 |
| 4 | France | 234.8 | 4 | France | 228.8 |
| 5 | United Kingdom | 205 | 5 | United Kingdom | 227.2 |
| 6 | Italy | 189.5 | 6 | Italy | 167.5 |
| 7 | Canada | 165.4 | 7 | Canada | 155.1 |
| 8 | Netherlands | 155.1 | 8 | Netherlands | 139.4 |
| 9 | Belgium-Luxembourg | 140.1 | 9 | Belgium-Luxembourg | 131 |
| 10 | China | 121 | 10 | China | 115.7 |
| 11 | Korea | 96 | 11 | Korea | 102.3 |
| 12 | Taiwan | 92.9 | 12 | Spain | 92.2 |
| 13 | Spain | 73.1 | 13 | Taiwan | 85.5 |
| 14 | Switzerland | 70.3 | 14 | Mexico | 81.5 |
| 15 | Sweden | 61.3 | 15 | Switzerland | 67.9 |
| Memo: | Hong Kong | | Memo: | Hong Kong | |
| | Total exports | 151.5 | | Total imports | 165.9 |
| | Domestic exports | 28.7 | | Retained imports | 43.2 |
| | Re-exports | 122.7 | | | |

*Source:* World Trade Organization.

China has also become a significant importer (see Table 2.7). Though its growth in this area has not been as dramatic as its growth in exports, China is a substantial export market for a number of countries (see Table 2.8). As would be expected given its rapid industrialization, many of China's imports tend to be products such as electrical machinery, aircraft, and nuclear reactors that are used to build infrastructure and a manufacturing base. Components for assembly and re-export are another major element of China's imports. China also imports substantial fertilizer and agricultural products, which go to support the nutritional needs of its citizens. Some estimate that China will be forced increasingly to rely upon imports for agricultural products and energy in the next decade.[39] On the whole, however, though spe-

Table 2.8

**China's Major Import Sources, as Reported by China, 1995**
($million and percent)

|  | Imports | Share of total |
|---|---|---|
| Japan | 29.007 | 22.0% |
| United States | 16,123 | 12.2% |
| Taiwan | 14,785 | 11.2% |
| Korea | 10,288 | 7.8% |
| Hong Kong | 8,599 | 6.5% |
| Germany | 8,035 | 6.1% |
| Russia | 3,799 | 2.9% |
| Singapore | 3,398 | 2.6% |
| Italy | 3,116 | 2.4% |
| France | 2,649 | 2.0% |
| Australia | 2,585 | 2.0% |
| Canada | 2,243 | 1.7% |
| Malaysia | 2,065 | 1.6% |
| Indonesia | 2,053 | 1.6% |
| United Kingdom | 1,972 | 1.5% |
| Thailand | 1,611 | 1.2% |
| Belgium-Luxembourg | 1,148 | 0.9% |

*Source:* International Monetary Fund.

cific product category totals may vary, the overall pattern of China's imports is not likely to change much in the short term.

China's sources of imports follow investment patterns fairly closely. Again, Hong Kong and Taiwan are leading sources. The United States, Japan, and Europe are also major sources of imports and major investors. Japan's exports have risen sharply in recent years for reasons previously described. The U.S. share of the Chinese market declined in the 1990s for reasons analyzed in the next section.

Initially, China's global trade balance raises no serious concerns. It has shifted from relatively small surpluses to small deficits and back. The enormous surpluses run up by Japan have not emerged. This initial impression is, however, quite deceptive. The missing element in the equation is that China has been growing at a double-digit rate during the 1990s. In periods of rapid growth, economies generally draw in large amounts of imports

Figure 2.5.  **Trade Balances and Economic Growth in China (1988–1995) and Japan (1963–1970)**

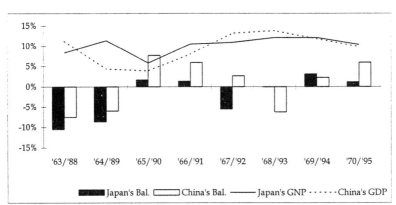

*Source:* IMF.

and run sizable trade deficits. This was certainly the case with Mexico, and even South Korea, which is renowned for its protectionism, has run a sizable trade deficit in recent years.[40]

Some observers point to the fact that China's global trade surplus has not approached that of Japan as evidence that China is not a mercantilist.[41] This comparison is simply inappropriate, however. China in the 1990s cannot reasonably be compared to Japan in the 1980s, despite the attempts of some commentators. China is a rapidly industrializing and rapidly growing economy in the 1990s; Japan was already developed and was experiencing relatively slow growth in the 1980s. If China is compared to Japan in the 1960s, when Japan was industrializing and growing at a double-digit rate, the parallel is undeniable (see Figure 2.5). In fact, China has actually run larger surpluses than Japan at comparable periods. A comparison to South Korea in the 1970s and 1980s demonstrates similar parallels (see Figure 2.6).

The apparent similarities between the trade patterns of China and Japan is of concern for two reasons. In light of China's rapid growth, imports are considerably lower than expected. The experience with Japan would indicate that once this period of rapid growth slows, as it presumably will at some point, imports will

Figure 2.6. **Trade Balances and Economic Growth in China (1984–1995) and Korea (1968–1979)**

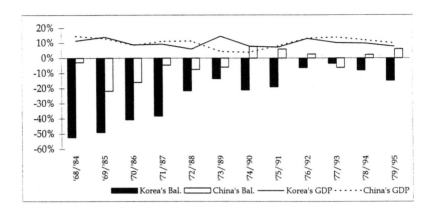

*Source:* IMF.

slow even more and China will likely tally enormous surpluses similar to those of Japan.[42] The enormous Japanese trade surpluses have put a significant economic burden upon the world economy and a great political strain on the global trading system. If China does emerge as a second Japan, the combined impact on the global economy and the trading system could be quite serious.

Despite a relatively balanced global trade account, China is already running trade surpluses with the "Big 3" trading powers —the United States, Japan, and the EU. The United States has imported much more from China, exported less, and, as a result, run a much larger bilateral trade deficit with China than the others (see Figures 2.7–2.9). The higher level of imports into the United States is not too surprising. Although there is some debate over which economy is the most open, most seem to feel that the United States is the most open large economy in the world. A WTO review of U.S. trade practices generally confirmed this conclusion. Further, the U.S. consumer market is large and has proven a lucrative target for most export-oriented Asian economies, including South Korea, Taiwan, Indonesia, and Japan.

**Figure 2.7. EU-12, Japanese, and U.S. Exports to China, 1987–1995 ($billion)**

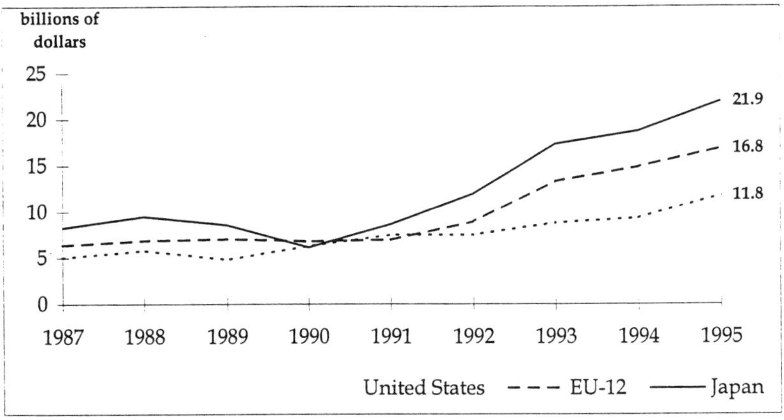

Sources: Ministry of Finance, Eurostat, Department of Commerce.

The poor performance of U.S. exports is somewhat surprising. U.S. exports to China have grown well in 1995 and 1996, but the 1990s have seen an overall erosion in the United States export market share in China. For example, in 1990, the United States exported more to China than Japan. By 1994, Japan was exporting twice as much to China as the United States. In light of favorable movement of the dollar against the yen during this period and the competitiveness of U.S. capital good exports, this erosion in U.S. export performance is all the more difficult to explain.

Two factors probably help to explain the weak U.S. export performance. First, the United States has at several points held up export financing to China and has barred China from many of its aid programs.[43] At the same time, Japan and Europe have aggressively and generously extended both of these programs to China. Japan's efforts to extend aid to China and simultaneously create opportunities for Japanese companies are of particular note. Though it is hard to assign a figure to this factor, in terms of lost U.S. exports, it does seem to be significant.

A second factor contributing to weak U.S. export performance

Figure 2.8.  **EU-12, Japanese, and U.S. Imports from China, 1987–1995** ($billion)

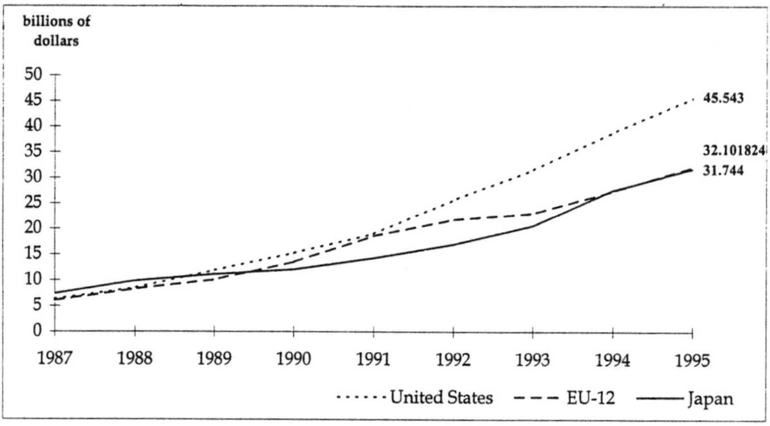

Sources: Ministry of Finance, Eurostat, Department of Commerce.

has been the ongoing political tension between the United States and China. In its role as a world leader, the United States has been prominent in criticizing China for violation of human rights, arms sales, piracy of intellectual property, and a raft of other issues. This has led to significant ongoing tensions between the United States and China and claims from China that the United States was seeking to "contain" Chinese influence.[44] The U.S. Congress, in an effort to apply leverage on these issues, has also threatened to impose high tariffs on Chinese exports to the United States.[45] The combined effect of all these tensions has been to insert acrimony and uncertainty into the U.S.-China relationship, which can only damage U.S. export prospects.

The direct result of growing Chinese exports to the United States and low Chinese imports from the United States has been a burgeoning U.S. trade deficit with China. In June of 1996, the monthly bilateral U.S. deficit with China surpassed the U.S. deficit with Japan to become the leading source of the U.S. trade deficit. Japan had previously been the largest source of the U.S. trade deficit in each month since April 1978.[46]

Although its growth slowed in the first half of 1996, the Chi-

**Figure 2.9. EU-12, Japanese, and U.S. Trade Balances with China, 1987–1995 ($billion)**

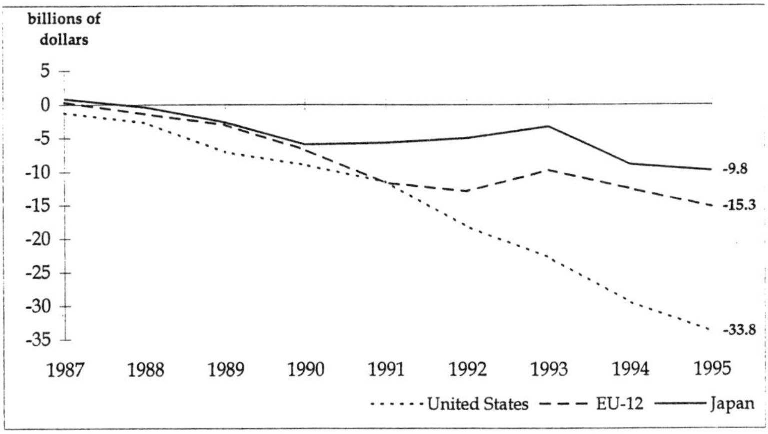

*Sources:* Ministry of Finance, Eurostat, Department of Commerce.

nese bilateral trade surplus with the United States continues to expand. Given the much higher volume of Chinese exports to the United States than imports from the United States, even if imports from the United States grow, the bilateral deficit is likely to expand. Further, as a result of appreciation of the yen, Japanese off-shoring of manufacturing capacity, and increased U.S. exports to Japan, the U.S. bilateral deficit with Japan is shrinking.[47] The result of these two trends is that China will likely soon pass Japan to become the largest source of the U.S. trade deficit for the entire year (see Figure 2.10).

Concerned that the rising trade imbalance with the United States would lead to increased Sino-U.S. tensions, Chinese officials and some others have argued that the bilateral deficit should be ignored. Essentially, they argue that the rising U.S. trade deficit is the result of a shifting of the trade surplus from other economies, notably that of Hong Kong.[48]

This position is, however, not very persuasive. It is certainly true that a number of countries have shifted some manufacturing to China because of labor costs and have, thus, replaced exports

Figure 2.10.  U.S. Trade Balances with China and Japan, 1980–1996 ($billion)

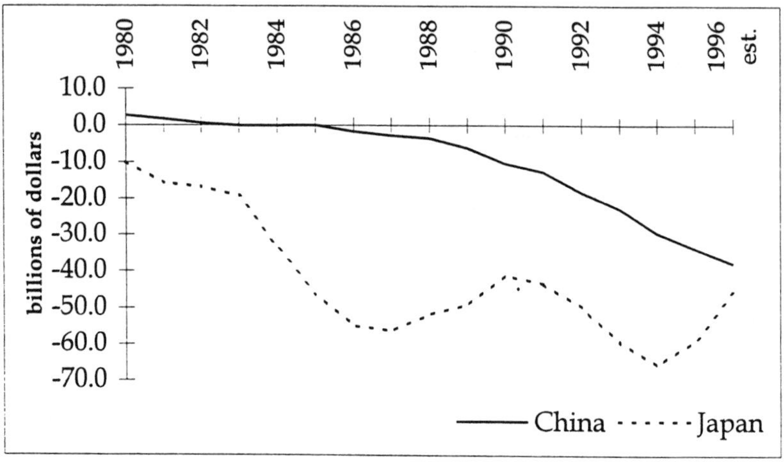

Source: Department of Commerce and ESI estimates.

from the home country with exports from China. This has been the case with Taiwan and may well become the case with Japan. There is more to the story, however. As is explained in Chapter 6, much of this exporting is the result of Chinese requirements that foreign firms export from facilities in China. In addition, China is simply displacing the exports of many of its neighbors in international markets because of its strong comparative advantage; the shifting deficit is often not a case of manufacturing investments shifting but the competitiveness of Chinese exports. For example, Korea's exports have clearly suffered as China has emerged as an exporting power. Some Korean firms are investing in China but probably not enough to account for the entire decline.[49] Further, the foreign exchange earned from exports to the United States should allow China to finance increased imports regardless of the country of origin of the owner of the exporting facility. But China's imports have grown more slowly than expected, due, at least in part, to Chinese mercantilism.

The argument that Hong Kong is responsible for the U.S. trade deficit with China is particularly unpersuasive. Some observers rightly point out that many of China's exports move through Hong Kong and contain Hong Kong input.[50] On the other side of the ledger, the argument continues, some U.S. exports, eventually destined for China, pass through Hong Kong and are counted by U.S. customs authorities as exports to Hong Kong and not China. There is truth in both of these arguments, but the customs counting procedures applied to Hong Kong and China are the same as those applied to all other countries. Almost all manufactured products in international trade contain input from more than one country. For example, U.S. auto imports from Canada and Mexico contain substantial Japanese input, yet are counted as Canadian or Mexican imports. Customs authorities around the world make similar, admittedly arbitrary, decisions on nation of origin of exports. These decisions are not unique to China, and China has no claim for special treatment.

Further, these same observers do not address one obvious implication of their approach. Namely, that many U.S. imports from Hong Kong also presumably contain some Chinese input. In other words, just as China's exports contain some Hong Kong input, Hong Kong's exports often contain some Chinese input. For example, many items of apparel exported from Hong Kong are made from Chinese textiles. If Hong Kong's exports were adjusted as the critics propose doing for China's exports through Hong Kong, the result would be additional exports being attributed to China and a larger U.S.-China bilateral trade imbalance.

Finally, control of Hong Kong shifts to Beijing in the summer of 1997.[51] With power in the hands of Beijing, it seems to be of little use to even make a distinction between Chinese exports and Hong Kong exports. Chinese authorities could clearly manipulate origin to make the distinction meaningless and, given the focus on the bilateral deficit, have every incentive to do exactly that if a distinction is made. The wisest course seems to be simply aggregating Hong Kong and Chinese exports to the United States. If this adjustment is made, the overall size of the U.S.-China trade imbalance is essentially unchanged (see Figure 2.11).

Trade deficits are not the best indicator of protectionism and

Figure 2.11.  U.S. Trade Balances with Hong Kong and China, 1980–1995

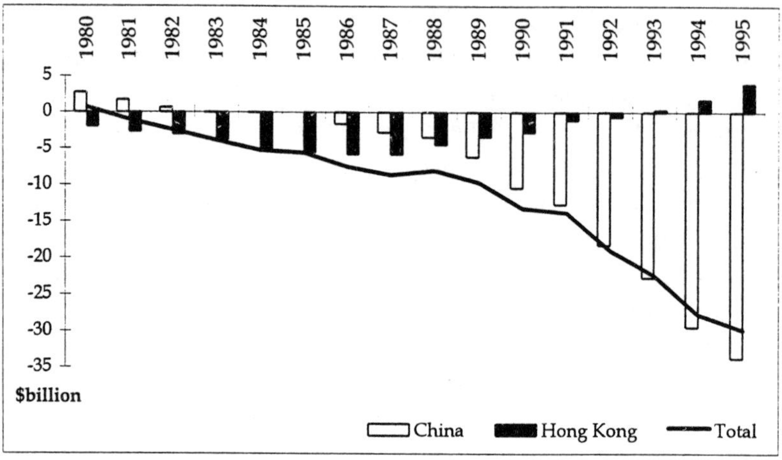

*Source:* Bureau of the Census.

mercantilism. Under the correct economic conditions, protection-ist countries, such as South Korea, can run a trade deficit. Under other conditions, a completely open market can run a trade sur-plus. Nonetheless, China's bilateral trade surpluses with Europe, Japan, and particularly the United States are large enough to constitute real signs of trouble. China's recent global trade sur-pluses, run while growing at a double-digit rate, are an even more telling trouble indicator for the future. Overall, China's trade performance shows every sign of China's developing into a new persistent trade surplus country, in the pattern of Japan.

**Foreign Borrowing and Aid**

The discussion to this point would give most readers the impres-sion that FDI and exports were the only sources of capital for the Chinese economy. Though they may be the most noteworthy sources of funds, they are not the only ones. China also has access to significant capital through foreign borrowing and aid.

Despite a disruption in the flow of World Bank lending and

Table 2.9

**World Bank Lending Activity to China, 1980–1994 ($million)**

|      | Commitments | | | Disbursements | | |
| --- | --- | --- | --- | --- | --- | --- |
|      | Total | IBRD | IDA | Total | IBRD | IDA |
| 1980 | —     | —     | —    | —     | —    | —   |
| 1981 | 196   | 100   | 96   | —     | —    | —   |
| 1982 | 330   | 165   | 165  | 1     | —    | 1   |
| 1983 | 438   | 299   | 139  | 71    | 4    | 67  |
| 1984 | 959   | 616   | 343  | 197   | 73   | 124 |
| 1995 | 1,093 | 660   | 433  | 566   | 354  | 212 |
| 1996 | 1,120 | 672   | 448  | 606   | 324  | 282 |
| 1987 | 1,305 | 692   | 613  | 702   | 303  | 399 |
| 1988 | 1,462 | 868   | 594  | 1,110 | 553  | 557 |
| 1989 | 1,760 | 1,221 | 539  | 1,111 | 604  | 507 |
| 1990 | 953   | 75    | 878  | 1,098 | 591  | 507 |
| 1991 | 2,622 | 1,312 | 1,310 | 1,280 | 668  | 612 |
| 1992 | 1,865 | 1,253 | 612  | 1,330 | 552  | 778 |
| 1993 | 2,315 | 1,445 | 870  | 1,846 | 977  | 869 |
| 1994 | 4,077 | 2,987 | 1,090 | 2,060 | 1,380 | 680 |

*Source:* World Bank, *The Chinese Economy: Fighting Inflation, Deepening Reforms, 1996.*

some continuing restrictions resulting from U.S. policy after Tiananmen Square,[52] China is, far and away, the largest borrower from the World Bank (see Table 2.9). This lending generally has below-market terms and is devoted to building infrastructure projects, such as roads, dams, and so forth. In the aftermath of Tiananmen, the United States has pressed for all new World Bank lending to be related to humanitarian projects, projects that improve the lives of average Chinese citizens.

China is also the largest borrower from the Asian Development Bank (ADB), which funds similar projects on a regional basis. ADB lending is not constrained by the same limits as the World Bank, however, because the United States is not a donor and other donors have not insisted upon a humanitarian restriction. Japan is the largest donor to the ADB.

China has pursued a much more conservative borrowing strategy than most developing countries, insisting that export earnings more than cover foreign borrowing. According to World Bank figures, in 1994, China's total foreign borrowing approached $120 billion, with about $30 billion of that total official borrowing. For comparison, Indonesia borrowed only slightly less, with an economy a fraction the size of China's.

Credit for most of China's import transactions is provided by national export financing agencies in the exporting country, like the U.S. Export–Import Bank (see Table 2.10). Total borrowing from this source stood at about $18 billion in 1995. For its part, the U.S. Export–Import Bank suspended lending to China after Tiananmen Square and again for several months in 1996 over a dispute with China on sales of nuclear technology.[53] The Export–Import Bank has also declined to finance U.S. exports to the largest infrastructure project in China, the Three Gorges Dam project, because of environmental concerns.[54] Except for a brief disruption after Tiananmen Square, other national lending agencies have generally not imposed similar restrictions. Given China's level of development and the size of its export market, it is not at all surprising that it is the major borrower of national export financing funds.

China also borrows some funds from commercial banks (see Table 2.11). Given its size and growth rate, China could borrow substantially more to finance imports for infrastructure development and other purposes. As noted in the previous section, however, China has not followed a typical "borrow to import" development pattern.

In addition to lending, much of which is at below-market terms, China receives substantial developmental aid from national governments, also known as overseas development assistance (ODA) (see Table 2.12). China is the world's leading recipient of such aid, taking in some $3.5 billion in ODA in 1994. Although most of this aid is not formally tied to purchasing products from the donor governments, few would deny that this has been a primary objective of donor governments. Japan has been noted in particular for using its aid programs to gain entry for Japanese companies and products. Again, as a result of

Table 2.10

**Projects and Purchases Facilitated by Export–Import Bank Loans to China, 1995**

| Purpose | Principal supplier | Loans ($million) | Guarantees ($million) |
|---|---|---|---|
| Air separation plant | Air Products and Chemicals | 21,059 | |
| Dadong power plant | Sargent Lundy Engineers | 233,413 | |
| Dalian power plant | Sargent Lundy Engineers | 197,851 | |
| Airport expansion | ARINC Research Corporation | 25,415 | |
| Shearing lines | Littell International, Inc. | 11,116 | |
| Passenger aircraft | Boeing Company | | 80,700 |
| Passenger aircraft | Boeing Company | | 69,996 |
| Passenger aircraft | Boeing Company | | 108,732 |
| Passenger aircraft | Boeing Company | | 28,378 |
| Telephone switching equipment | AT&T | | 20,673 |

*Source*: 1995 Annual Report of Export–Import Bank.

Table 2.11

**China's Disbursements of Loans from Private Sources, 1987–1994**
($billions)

|  | Bonds | Commercial banks | Other private | Private non-guaranteed | Private credits |
|---|---|---|---|---|---|
| 1987 | 1.1 | 4.6 | 1.3 | 0.0 | 6.9 |
| 1988 | 0.8 | 4.5 | 2.0 | 0.0 | 7.2 |
| 1989 | 0.5 | 2.0 | 3.2 | 0.0 | 5.7 |
| 1990 | 0.3 | 3.2 | 3.6 | 0.0 | 7.1 |
| 1991 | 0.3 | 2.6 | 3.1 | 0.0 | 6.0 |
| 1992 | 0.9 | 5.1 | 7.2 | 0.2 | 13.4 |
| 1993 | 2.7 | 5.6 | 5.4 | 0.3 | 14.1 |
| 1994 | 3.3 | 3.6 | 7.1 | 0.0 | 14.1 |

*Source:* World Bank.

Table 2.12

**Largest Recipients of Overseas Development Assistance (ODA),
1990–1994** ($billion)

|  | 1990 | 1991 | 1992 | 1993 | 1994* | 1990–1994 |
|---|---|---|---|---|---|---|
| China | 2.2 | 2.0 | 3.1 | 3.3 | 3.5 | 14.1 |
| Egypt | 5.4 | 5.0 | 3.6 | 3.3 | 2.3 | 19.6 |
| Indonesia | 1.7 | 1.9 | 2.1 | 2.0 | 2.2 | 9.9 |
| India | 1.5 | 2.7 | 2.4 | 1.5 | 1.4 | 9.5 |
| Bangladesh | 2.0 | 1.6 | 1.7 | 1.4 | 1.3 | 8.0 |

*Source:* World Bank.
*1994 totals are estimates by World Bank and OECD staff.

Tiananmen Square sanctions, the United States does not extend its equivalent program, tied development aid or TDA, to China.[55]

## Conclusion

Sadly, in relying heavily upon statistics, tables, and charts to paint a picture of events, as is the case with this chapter, there is a danger that the flood of details and statistics will obscure the big picture. That would be unfortunate indeed in this case, because the statistics of this chapter lay out one of the most fascinating economic developments in recent history.

When historians look back upon the twentieth century, the meteoric rise of the Chinese economy will undoubtedly be among its most important events. In light of the considerable political and security implications of a more powerful China, China's rise to economic superpower status could effect world affairs in many ways, some positive and some negative.

China's economic surge has materially changed the lives of most if not all of its 1.3 billion citizens. The booming industrial base on China's coast has changed the flow of trade and commerce, not only in the region, but also throughout the world. China's economic development has also made it a far more important force in world affairs in all spheres, military and diplomatic as well as economic. By most accounts, China is already one of the world's three largest economies. If current trends continue for even another decade, it will challenge the United States as the world's largest economy. At that point, the trends just mentioned will grow even more noteworthy.

What is not known, however, is whether or not these developments will prove beneficial for the world economy and world affairs generally. It is possible that China's economic success will come at the cost of other countries victimized by Chinese mercantilism. It is possible that growing Chinese economic strength will embolden China and make it a more aggressive and disruptive influence in world affairs. From a more optimistic perspective, it is also possible that China will be efficiently integrated into the world economy in a way that improves both China and the world. Ultimately, the question that will face historians is whether the economic rise of China was a positive or a negative development. The primary purpose of this book is to isolate specific problems and suggest steps that could be taken to encourage China to evolve in a positive direction.

## Notes

1. Real growth rates are based on statistics on the country pages of the International Monetary Fund's *International Financial Statistics Yearbook,*

*1995* (Washington, DC: International Monetary Fund, 1995), hereafter referred to as *IFS*.

2. Some have speculated that growth might slow further in 1997; however, given the many uncertainties about the Chinese economy, such predictions are little more than guesswork.

3. From 1979 to 1991, the cumulative value for FDI contracts was $50.4 billion. In 1992 and 1993, FDI contracts totaled $58.1 billion and $111.4 billion, respectively.

4. United Nations Conference on Trade and Development, Division on Transnational Corporations and Investment, *World Investment Report, 1996* (Geneva and New York: United Nations, 1996).

5. Nicholas R. Lardy, *China in the World Economy* (Washington, DC: Institute for International Economics, 1994), 4 and 5*n*.

6. China's exports have grown from $27.6 billion in 1985 to $148.8 billion in 1995.

7. For instance, inward FDI data is inflated by the tendency of foreign firms to overvalue their equipment investment and by domestic investors channeling capital through foreign countries in order to benefit from government incentives. See United Nations Conference on Trade and Development, Division on Transnational Corporations and Investment, *World Investment Report, 1995: Transnational Corporations and Competitiveness* (Geneva and New York: United Nations, 1995), 59–60. China underreports its exports to industrial countries because it classifies trade that passes through Hong Kong ports as trade with Hong Kong. See *Direction of Trade Statistics Yearbook, 1996* (Washington, DC: International Monetary Fund, 1996), 159.

8. For descriptions of the various methodologies used to measure China's GNP, see World Bank, China and Mongolia Department, "China: GNP per Capita," Report No. 13399–CHA (Washington, DC: World Bank, 1994).

9. Ibid.

10. In 1994, saving and investment amounted to about 40 percent of China's nominal GDP. See World Bank, *The Chinese Economy—Fighting Inflation, Deepening Reforms* (Washington, DC: The World Bank, 1996), 72.

11. "Ninth Five-Year Plan: A Watershed for China," *Chemical Week*, August 28, 1996, S6–S10.

12. Lester R. Brown and Hsal Kane, *Reassessing the Earth's Population Carrying Capacity* (Washington, DC: Worldwatch Institute, 1995).

13. Kent E. Calder, "Asia's Empty Gas Tank," *Foreign Affairs* (March/April 1996), 55–60.

14. Based on *IFS* statistics, China's total goods and services trade-to-GDP ratios are lower than corresponding ratios for Indonesia, Malaysia, Thailand, the Philippines, and Korea.

15. Greg Mastel, *Trading with the Middle Kingdom* (Washington, DC: Economic Strategy Institute, 1995), 35.

16. Relatively more sophisticated manufactured exports from the machinery and transport equipment sectors accounted for 18 percent of China's merchandise exports in 1994.

17. Jim Rowher, "The Titan Stirs," *Economist,* November 28, 1992, 3–8.

18. Lardy, *China in the World Economy,* 24.

19. World Bank, *The Chinese Economy,* 8, 108.

20. World Bank, *China: Foreign Trade Reform* (Washington, DC: The World Bank, 1994), 11.

21. Prepared statement of Ambassador Winston Lord, Assistant Secretary of State for East Asian and Pacific Affairs, before the Senate Committee on Foreign Relations Subcommittee on East Asian and Pacific Affairs, July 18, 1996.

22. Harry Harding, *A Fragile Relationship: The United States and China since 1972* (Washington, DC: The Brookings Institution, 1992), 67–87.

23. "More Money Sent to China by Taiwan Residents," *Agence France-Presse,* August 28, 1996.

24. By the early 1990s, for instance, Japanese manufacturers were far less internationalized than their U.S. and European counterparts. See Edward J. Lincoln, *Japan's New Global Role* (Washington, DC: The Brookings Institution, 1993), 65–67.

25. William Dawkins, "Yen's Rise Prompts Exodus," *Financial Times,* July 3, 1996, 2.

26. Christopher P. Johnstone, "Japan's Foreign Aid: New Approach, New Controversy," JEI Report No. 40 A (Washington, DC: Japan Economic Institute, 1996), 8–12.

27. Greg Mastel, "Baffling U.S. Trade Policy," *Journal of Commerce,* September 13, 1996.

28. Richard Johnson and James B. Teece, "Big 3 Find Dealings in China Sweet, Sour: Chrysler Minivan Deal Appears Dead," *Automotive News,* May 8, 1995, 3.

29. Rajiv Chandrasekaran, "Motorola's Next Page; The Cellular Giant and Onetime Star Seeks Ways to Renew Its Growth," *Washington Post,* September 29, 1996.

30. Josephine Ma, "Foreign Companies Find Insurance Can Be a Risky Venture," *South China Morning Post,* November 14, 1996, 1.

31. United States Trade Representative, *1996 National Trade Estimate Report on Foreign Trade Barriers* (Washington, DC: U.S. Government Printing Office, 1996), 56–57.

32. China was the world's eleventh largest exporter in 1994, but according to the WTO, 78 percent of exports from Hong Kong, the ninth largest exporter, were re-exports passing through its port. Appropriately adjusting Hong Kong's exports to reflect what it actually manufactures bumps China up to number ten on the list. See World Trade Organization, Economic Research and Analysis Division and the Statistics and Information Systems Division, "International Trade Trends and Statistics" (Brussels: World Trade Organization, 1995), Table 1.7.

33. Lardy, *China in the World Economy,* 18–25.

34. According to statistics from the United Nations Comtrade Database, 86 percent of China's exports in 1995 were classified as manufactured goods.

35. According to statistics from the United Nations Comtrade Database, China's exports of SITC Rev. 3 No. 778 grew from $838 million in 1992 to $2.43 billion in 1995.

36. Lewis M. Simons, "High Tech Jobs for Sale," *Time,* July 22, 1996, 59–60.

37. Mastel, *Trading with the Middle Kingdom,* 35.

38. For a discussion of some recent issues related to this topic see Paula Green, "China-U.S. Textile Pact Tailors Quota of Imports," *Journal of Commerce,* February 6, 1997, 2A.

39. Calder, "Asia's Empty Gas Tank," 58–60; and Brown and Kane, *Reassessing.*

40. From 1989 to 1995, Korea's cumulative merchandise trade deficit was $33.6 billion.

41. Lardy, *China in the World Economy,* 35–37.

42. Lawrence H. Sumners, Undersecretary of Treasury for International Affairs, testimony before the Senate Banking, Housing, and Urban Affairs Committee, May 25, 1993.

43. See, for instance, Paul Blustein and R. Jeffrey Smith, "Economic, Political Concerns Put Clinton on the Spot in China," *Washington Post,* February 11, 1996.

44. Simon Beck, "Poll Shows Image Plunge in U.S.," *South China Morning Post,* February 12, 1996.

45. Mastel, *Trading with the Middle Kingdom,* 37–39.

46. "U.S. Trade Gap Is Now Biggest with Chinese," *Plain Dealer,* August 21, 1996.

47. According to U.S. Department of Commerce statistics, the U.S. trade deficit with Japan for the first eight months of 1996 was 28 percent below year earlier levels.

48. Lardy, *China in the World Economy,* 73–79.

49. Korean exports of "apparel and other textile products" (SIC 23) and "leather and leather products" (SIC 31) have been hit especially hard. U.S. imports of these products from Korea dropped $2.9 billion between 1989 and 1994. It is possible that some firms based in third countries shifted plants from Korea to China.

50. Lardy, *China in the World Economy,* 73–79.

51. At midnight, June 30, 1997, Hong Kong will become a Special Administrative Region of the People's Republic of China.

52. Greg Mastel, "Baffling U.S. Trade Policy."

53. Blustein and Smith, "Economic, Political Concerns," 4.

54. Ibid.

55. Lardy, *China in the World Economy,* 97–98.

# 3

# Overview of the Chinese Political System

This book primarily addresses economic issues and economic policy questions concerning China; it is not a discussion of Chinese politics and China's government. Nonetheless, in order to gain a full understanding of key economic issues, it is important to be familiar with both the political situation and the basic policymaking institutions in China. This chapter attempts to meet those needs, but if the reader is interested primarily in those issues, he or she will probably want to look elsewhere.

Even a cursory discussion of this topic is difficult because the Chinese political system is not transparent; much occurs behind closed doors, out of the public eye, and certainly away from western eyes. It is usually possible to obtain formal organizational charts of the Chinese government, but these tell, at most, only part of the story. Observers of the Chinese political system often emphasize the importance of shifting alliances between senior officials and family ties over positions on organizational charts. The Chinese system is particularly difficult for westerners to understand because what appear to be promotions can often, in fact, be demotions. There is a long tradition in China of leaders promoting rivals to "brightly lit shelves," highly visible positions with no real power.[1]

Further, the record of China watchers in predicting events in China has not been good. Much emphasis is often given to recounting who spoke to whom at public events, positions on rostrums, and cryptic comments in the press.[2] In the end, it often seems that China watchers are doing little more than repeating Beijing rumors, which are about as accurate as rumors in other national capitals, hardly reliable predictors of future events.

Nonetheless, in order to predict the future course of China's economic policies and economic trends, it is necessary to make some assumptions about the longevity of the current Chinese regime and its policies. It is also important to understand the key party and government bodies as well as the key economic agencies within the Chinese government.

## Key Central Institutions

China's communist heritage is most clearly seen in the organization of its central government. Power is exercised by five primary bodies: (1) the Politburo, (2) the political leadership of the national government, (3) the National People's Congress, (4) commissions and ministries, and (5) the military.

### *The Politburo*

Under the shifting winds of Chinese politics, the power and influence of some entities, like the military and the National People's Congress, waxes and wanes. But true to its communist roots, the Communist Party's Central Committee and its Politburo remain at the heart of power in China (see Figures 3.1a and 3.1b).

The Central Committee has 186 full members and 130 alternate members. The decision-making body within the Central Committee is the Politburo. Typically, the Central Committee merely endorses the decisions of the Politburo.

The heart of the Politburo is its seven-member Standing Committee led by General Secretary Jiang Zemin. The other members of the Standing Committee are, in order of position: Li Peng, Qiao Shi, Li Ruihuan, Zhu Rongji, Liu Huaqing, and Hu Jintao.

The men now most frequently named as potential rivals to Jiang Zemin for power in the Chinese system, Li Peng, Qiao Shi,

Figure 3.1a. **Chinese Communist Party Organizations**

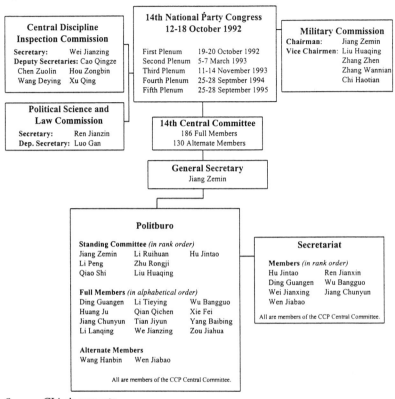

*Source:* CIA documents.
*Note:* Information as of March 1996.

and Liu Huaquing, are currently all members of the Standing Committee. In recent years, however, Jiang Zemin has been successful in bringing more of his personal allies onto the Politburo and the Standing Committee.[3] As noted, major decisions must eventually be formally sanctioned at the upcoming Fifteenth Party Congress of the Chinese Communist Party, but Party Congress actions normally amount to only a formal endorsement of decisions that have already been reached by the Politburo. Of course, the Politburo's actual deliberations are not transparent, and any predictions about its future actions on these or other issues is ultimately just speculation.

Figure 3.1b. **Chinese Communist Party Committee: Politburo and Secretariat**

Politburo

**Standing Committee** *(in rank order)*

| Name | Pronunciation | Born | Bio |
|---|---|---|---|
| Jiang Zemin | *(jeeyahng)* | 1926 | President; General Secretary; Chairman, Party and State Military Commissions |
| Li Peng | *(lee)* | 1928 | Premier |
| Qiao Shi | *(cheeyow)* | 1924 | Chairman, National People's Congress (NPC) |
| Li Ruihuan | *(lee)* | 1934 | Chairman of Chinese People's Political Consultative Conference |
| Zhu Rongji | *(joo)* | 1928 | First Vice Premier |
| Liu Huaqing | *(leeyo)* | 1916 | Vice Chairman, Party Military Commission |
| Hu Jintao | *(hoo)* | 1942 | President, Central Party School; member of Secretariat |

**Full Members** *(in alphabetical order)*

| Name | Pronunciation | Born | Bio |
|---|---|---|---|
| Ding Guangen | *(ding)* | 1929 | Director, CCP Propaganda Department |
| Huang Ju | *(hwahng)* | 1939 | Mayor, Shanghai; secretary, Shanghai Municipal CCP |
| Jiang Chunyun | *(jeeyahng)* | 1930 | Shandong party secretary; member of Secretariat |
| Li Lanqing | *(lee)* | 1932 | Vice Premier |
| Li Tieying | *(lee)* | 1936 | State Councilor; Minister, State Commission for Restructuring the Economic System |
| Qian Qichen | *(cheeyen)* | 1928 | Vice Premier; Minister Foreign Affairs |
| Tian Jiyun | *(teeyen)* | 1929 | Vice Chairman, NPC Standing Committee |
| Wei Jianzing | *(way)* | 1931 | Secretary Discipline Inspection Committee; member of Secretariat |
| Wu Bangguo | *(woo)* | 1941 | Shanghai party secretary; member of Secretariat |
| Xie Fei | *(hsieh)* | 1932 | Guangdong party secretary |
| Yang Baibing | *(yahng)* | 1920 | [bio unknown] |
| Zou Jiahua | *(dzoe)* | 1927 | Vice Premier |

**Alternate Members** *(in alphabetical order)*

| Name | Pronunciation | Born | Bio |
|---|---|---|---|
| Wang Hanbin | *(wahng)* | 1925 | Vice Chairman, NPC Standing Committee |
| Wen Jiabao | *(won)* | 1942 | Member of Secretariat |

**Secretariat Members** *(in rank order)*

| Name | Pronunciation | Born | Bio |
|---|---|---|---|
| Hu Jintao | see above | | |
| Ding Guangen | " " | | |
| Wei Jianxing | " " | | |
| Wen Jiabao | " " | | |
| Ren Jianxin | *(run)* | 1925 | Secretary of CCP Political Science and Law Commission; President, Supreme People's Court |
| Wu Bangguo | see above | | |
| Jiang Chunyun | " " | | |

*Source:* CIA documents.

## Political Leadership of the National Government

Jiang Zemin also serves as China's president, the head-of-state position. Aside from the president and his vice-president, the most important central government organization is the State Council, led by Premier Li Peng. In addition to Li Peng, the State Council is made up of fifteen vice-premiers, state councilors, and

Table 3.1

**China: Leading Officials in the Government and State Council**

| | |
|---|---|
| President: | Jiang Zemin |
| Vice President: | Rong Yiren |
| | |
| State Council | |
| Premier: | Li Peng |
| | |
| Vice Premiers: | Jiang Chunyun |
| | Li Lanqing |
| | Qian Qichen |
| | Wu Bangguo |
| | Zhu Rongji |
| | Zou Jiahua |
| | |
| Councilors: | Chen Junsheng |
| | Chi Haotian |
| | Ismail Amat |
| | Li Guixian |
| | Li Tieying |
| | Luo Gan |
| | Peng Peiyun (f) |
| | Song Jian |
| Secretary General: | Luo Gan |

*Source:* CIA documents. Information as of February 1996.
(f) Official known to be female.

a secretary general (see Table 3.1). The State Council directs the activities of the other agencies of the Chinese central government, including commissions, ministries, and a range of other working organs and other organizations.

## The National People's Congress

China's national legislature is known as the National People's Congress (NPC). It is currently led by its chairman, Qiao Shi. Traditionally, the NPC has been merely a rubber-stamp legislature, approving the decisions of the Politburo and the State Council (see Figure 3.2). As is discussed in more detail in Chapter 6, however, the NPC has evolved into a somewhat more indepen-

Figure 3.2.  **Government of the People's Republic of China**

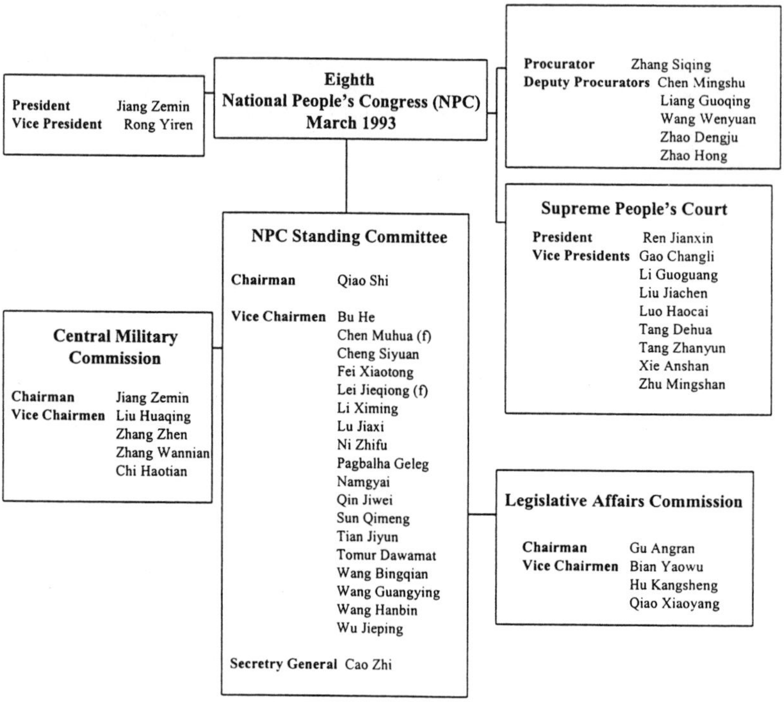

| | |
|---|---|
| **President** Jiang Zemin<br>**Vice President** Rong Yiren | **Eighth**<br>**National People's Congress (NPC)**<br>**March 1993** |

**Procurator** Zhang Siqing
**Deputy Procurators** Chen Mingshu
Liang Guoqing
Wang Wenyuan
Zhao Dengju
Zhao Hong

**NPC Standing Committee**

**Chairman**      Qiao Shi

**Vice Chairmen** Bu He
Chen Muhua (f)
Cheng Siyuan
Fei Xiaotong
Lei Jieqiong (f)
Li Ximing
Lu Jiaxi
Ni Zhifu
Pagbalha Geleg
Namgyai
Qin Jiwei
Sun Qimeng
Tian Jiyun
Tomur Dawamat
Wang Bingqian
Wang Guangying
Wang Hanbin
Wu Jieping

**Secretry General** Cao Zhi

**Central Military**
**Commission**

**Chairman**      Jiang Zemin
**Vice Chairmen** Liu Huaqing
Zhang Zhen
Zhang Wannian
Chi Haotian

**Supreme People's Court**

**President**      Ren Jianxin
**Vice Presidents** Gao Changli
Li Guoguang
Liu Jiachen
Luo Haocai
Tang Dehua
Tang Zhanyun
Xie Anshan
Zhu Mingshan

**Legislative Affairs Commission**

**Chairman**      Gu Angran
**Vice Chairmen** Bian Yaowu
Hu Kangsheng
Qiao Xiaoyang

*Source:* CIA documents.
*Note:* (f) Official known to be female.

dent body aimed at establishing the rule of law in China.
The NPC also has formal ties with a number of other Chinese
government institutions, including the Central Military Commission and the Supreme People's Court. In recent years, Qiao Shi
has argued for allowing the NPC to assume increased powers of
oversight of the Chinese military, but it remains to be seen
whether that will result in any changes.[4]

### Commissions and Ministries

Most day-to-day governing decisions are made by China's thirty-
one ministries and nine major commissions. These organizations

Figure 3.3. **Military Organizations of the People's Republic of China**

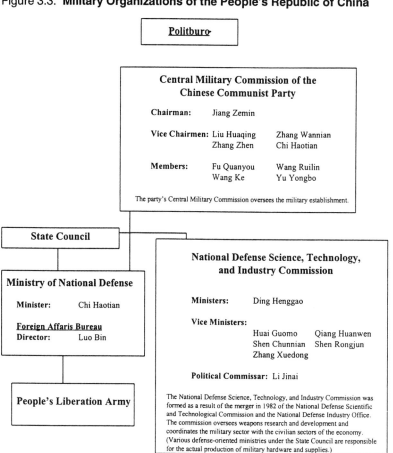

*Source:* CIA documents.
*Note:* Information as of March 1996.

are home to the government bureaucracy and the policy experts for particular issues. Most of these organizations are headed by members or alternate members of the Chinese Communist Party's Central Committee. Much of the operational responsibility for ministries is held by assistant ministers who are often career employees of the ministry.

*The Military*

No one doubts the continuing influence of the military within the Chinese government. Deng Xiaoping and Jiang Zemin are only the latest Chinese leaders to go to great pains to court the military. Although it is generally seen as inappropriate for one of China's generals to actually hold the top party or government posts, it is impossible for anyone to hold those posts without military support. On specific issues, such as handling of Taiwan policy, the military is also thought to hold sway (see Figure 3.3).[5]

Though its influence upon Chinese policy is considerable, there is little discussion of a military coup in China. There was, however, dissent within the military during the Tiananmen Square crisis.[6] This issue is discussed more fully in the closing section of this chapter (see Figure 3.4).

The military might seem initially to have little influence on economic and trade issues, but actually its role is significant. First, the military is seen as a conservative element within the Chinese government that is often skeptical about economic reforms, particularly those that may threaten the power of the state. Second, the military is a major direct player in the economy. The People's Liberation Army (PLA) operates a number of manufacturing facilities producing a wide range of products, including apparel, pots and pans, firearms, and aircraft parts.[7] The PLA's direct interest in the production and export of weapons and pirated intellectual property products has played an important role in U.S.-China disputes on these issues.

**Key Economic Policymaking Institutions**

The key economic institutions within the Chinese government are similar to those in all other governments: the central bank, the Ministry of Finance, and the Ministry of Trade. In addition, however, the state commissions that make up the planning apparatus of the communist government also play an important role in economic policy. Each of these organizations warrants a brief discussion (see Figure 3.5).

Figure 3.4.  **People's Liberation Army**

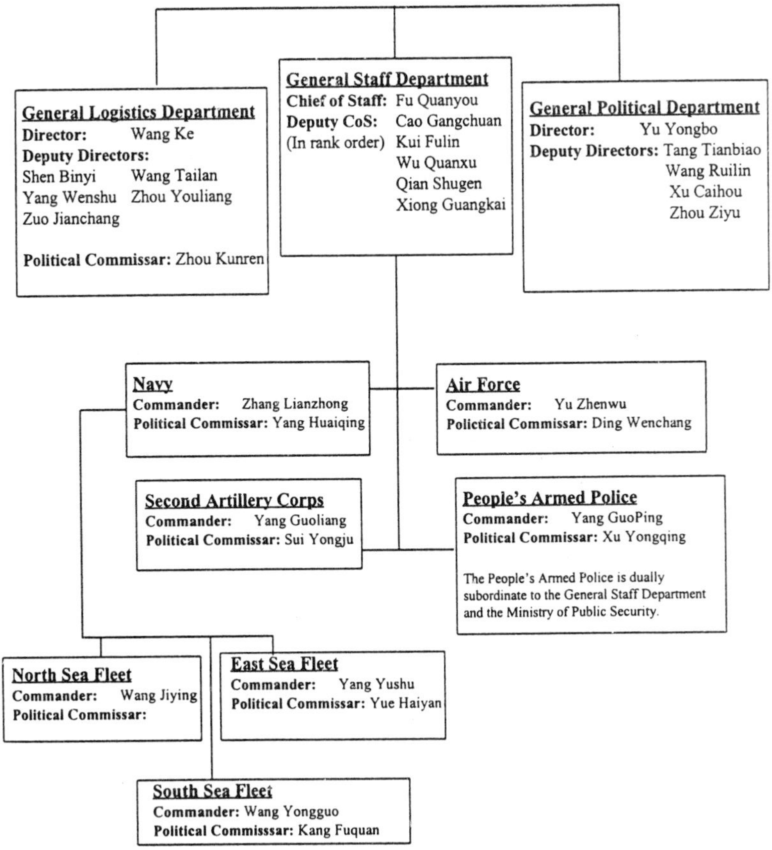

**General Logistics Department**
Director:       Wang Ke
Deputy Directors:
Shen Binyi      Wang Tailan
Yang Wenshu   Zhou Youliang
Zuo Jianchang

Political Commissar: Zhou Kunren

**General Staff Department**
Chief of Staff:  Fu Quanyou
Deputy CoS:    Cao Gangchuan
(In rank order) Kui Fulin
                Wu Quanxu
                Qian Shugen
                Xiong Guangkai

**General Political Department**
Director:        Yu Yongbo
Deputy Directors: Tang Tianbiao
                 Wang Ruilin
                 Xu Caihou
                 Zhou Ziyu

**Navy**
Commander:     Zhang Lianzhong
Political Commissar: Yang Huaiqing

**Air Force**
Commander:     Yu Zhenwu
Polictical Commissar: Ding Wenchang

**Second Artillery Corps**
Commander:     Yang Guoliang
Political Commissar: Sui Yongju

**People's Armed Police**
Commander:      Yang GuoPing
Political Commissar: Xu Yongqing

The People's Armed Police is dually
subordinate to the General Staff Department
and the Ministry of Public Security.

**North Sea Fleet**
Commander:     Wang Jiying
Political Commissar:

**East Sea Fleet**
Commander:     Yang Yushu
Political Commissar: Yue Haiyan

**South Sea Fleet**
Commander: Wang Yongguo
Political Commisssar: Kang Fuquan

*Source:* CIA documents.
*Note:* Information as of March 1996.

## The Ministry of Foreign Trade and Economic Cooperation

The Ministry of Foreign Trade and Economic Cooperation (MOFTEC) is China's trade ministry. It has primary responsibility for both foreign trade and investment policy. As part of its responsibilities, MOFTEC handles foreign trade negotiations, including negotiations on WTO accession (see Figure 3.6).

Figure 3.5.  **Key Economic Decision-Making Bodies**

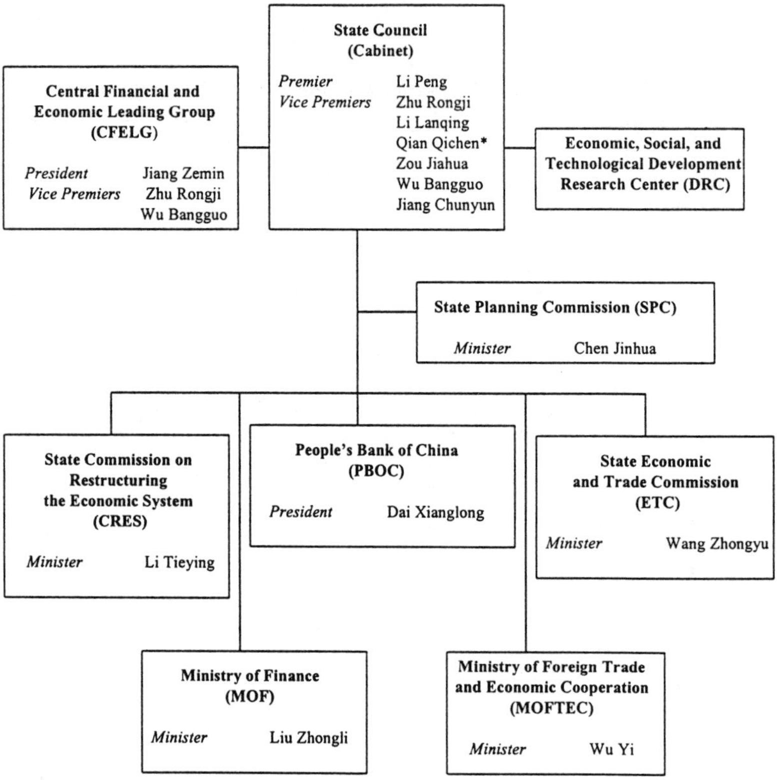

```
                          ┌─────────────────────┐
                          │    State Council    │
                          │     (Cabinet)       │
┌───────────────────────┐ │                     │
│ Central Financial and │ │ Premier      Li Peng│
│ Economic Leading Group│ │ Vice Premiers Zhu Rongji
│        (CFELG)        │ │              Li Lanqing
│                       │ │              Qian Qichen*  ┌──────────────────────────┐
│ President  Jiang Zemin│ │              Zou Jiahua    │ Economic, Social, and    │
│ Vice Premiers Zhu Rongji            Wu Bangguo      │ Technological Development │
│            Wu Bangguo │ │              Jiang Chunyun  │ Research Center (DRC)     │
└───────────────────────┘ └─────────────────────┘      └──────────────────────────┘

                          ┌──────────────────────────────────┐
                          │ State Planning Commission (SPC)   │
                          │                                   │
                          │ Minister        Chen Jinhua       │
                          └──────────────────────────────────┘

┌─────────────────────┐  ┌──────────────────────┐  ┌──────────────────────┐
│ State Commission on │  │ People's Bank of China│ │   State Economic     │
│   Restructuring     │  │       (PBOC)         │  │ and Trade Commission │
│ the Economic System │  │                      │  │        (ETC)         │
│      (CRES)         │  │ President Dai Xianglong│ │                      │
│                     │  └──────────────────────┘  │ Minister Wang Zhongyu│
│ Minister Li Tieying │                            └──────────────────────┘
└─────────────────────┘

                          ┌──────────────────────┐  ┌──────────────────────────┐
                          │ Ministry of Finance  │  │ Ministry of Foreign Trade│
                          │       (MOF)          │  │ and Economic Cooperation │
                          │                      │  │        (MOFTEC)          │
                          │ Minister Liu Zhongli │  │ Minister      Wu Yi      │
                          └──────────────────────┘  └──────────────────────────┘
```

*Source:* CIA documents.
Note: Information as of October 5, 1995.
* Not key player on economics; responsible for foreign affairs.

MOFTEC is a relatively new Chinese agency established in March of 1993. It is not considered one of China's more powerful agencies and is thought to have lost power struggles with the Ministry of Foreign Affairs, the State Planning Commission, the PLA, and other ministries on issues affecting international trade negotiations.

## The Ministry of Finance

China's Ministry of Finance is involved in policymaking on a range of finance and economic issues. The ministry plays a

Figure 3.6.  **The Ministry of Foreign Trade and Economic Cooperation (MOFTEC)**

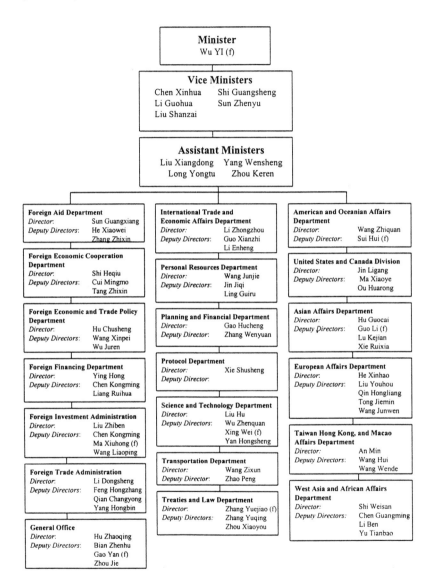

*Source:* CIA documents.

*Note:* (f) Official known to be female. Information as of April 1996.

prominent role on two issues discussed in some depth in this book, convertibility of the yuan and financing of SOEs.

## People's Bank of China

The People's Bank of China is China's central bank. As such, it plays a key role in setting exchange rates for the yuan against foreign currencies, regulating the money supply, setting interest rates, and other central bank functions.

In addition to the People's Bank, a number of other policy banks that lend funds for specific purposes—state and nationwide commercial banks, foreign banks, and nonbank financial institutions—comprise the Chinese banking system (see Table 3.2).

## The State Planning Commission

The State Planning Commission is the central organization for economic planning in China. It has ultimate responsibility for drafting both the five-year economic plans and the industry-specific plans, but these tasks are carried out in coordination with the relevant ministries. For example, in drafting the plan for the automotive industry, the State Planning Commission reportedly worked closely with both MOFTEC and the Ministry of Machinery, which is responsible for the automotive industry.[8]

Given its central role in the planning process and the relevance of this process to the WTO accession negotiations, a State Planning Commission representative was added to the team negotiating for China on WTO accession in Geneva.

This listing is by no means exhaustive but merely a brief description of the major Chinese agencies relevant to the topic of this book. Many others also play a role. For example, the State Economic and Trade Commission is involved in setting import demand.[9] The State Commission on Restructuring the Economic System plays a leading role in matters such as reform of the SOEs. The Ministry of Foreign Affairs is active in all international negotiations. As is discussed later, many of the individual

Table 3.2

## China's Financial System at a Glance

| Structure | Number of branches | Total assets (Renminbi billion) | Reforms |
|---|---|---|---|
| Banking system | | | |
| People's Bank of China | 2,529 | 1,758.8 | • 1978: People's Bank of China separated from Ministry of Finance. |
| Policy banks | | | • 1979: People's Construction Bank of |
| State Development Bank of China | — | 90.8 | China and Agricultural Bank of China re- |
| Agricultural Development Bank of China | — | 406.9 | established; China International Trust and |
| Export–Import Bank of China | — | 2.5 | Investment Corporation founded. The "Four Transformations" and Eight Reforms promulgated |
| State commercial banks | | | |
| Industrial and Commercial Bank of China | 37,039 | 2,633.9 | • 1981: Resumption of government domes- |
| Agricultural Bank of China | 63,816 | 1,253.1 | tic bonds issue. |
| Bank of China | 12,630 | 1,837.9 | |
| People's Construction Bank of China | 33,979 | 1,397.5 | • 1983: State Council decides to separate |
| Nationwide commercial banks | | | People's Insurance Company from |
| Bank of Communications | 1,937 | 305.0 | People's Bank of China; Industrial and |
| China Trust and Investment Corporation | | | Commercial Bank of China to take over |
| Industrial Bank | 54 | 70.7 | commercial banking business of PBC. |
| China Everbright Bank | 12 | 20.3 | |
| Hua Xia Bank | n.a. | 82.9 | |

*(continued)*

Table 3.2 (continued)

| Structure | Number of branches | Total assets (Renminbi billion) | Reforms |
|---|---|---|---|
| Mins Sheng (opening early 1996) | — | n.a. | • 1987: Bank of Communications reestablished; urban credit cooperatives, trust and investment corporations, and finance companies formally established |
| **Other commercial banks** | | | |
| China Investment Bank | 31 | 44.5 | |
| Guangdong Development Bank | 11 | 43.1 | • 1988: Secondary market for treasury bonds starts. |
| Shenzhen Development Bank | n.a. | 15.4 | |
| Pudong Development Bank | 18 | 17.8 | |
| Shenzhen Merchants Bank | 9 | 44.7 | |
| Fujian Industrial Bank | 7 | 19.8 | • 1990: Cutback in number of trust and investment corporations, finance companies; recognition of Shanghai Security Exchange. |
| Yantai Housing Saving Bank | 5 | n.a. | |
| Bengbu Housing Saving Bank | n.a. | n.a. | |
| **Nonbank financial institutions** | | | |
| Rural Credit Cooperatives | 50,745 | 505.3 | • 1993: Third Plenum of the 14th Central Committee of the Communist Party of China adopts its November "Decisions," announcing an acceleration of financial sector reforms. Main elements include: more independence for the People's Bank of China; greater interest rate flexibility; commercialization of specialized banks; establishment of policy banks; and payments system development. |
| Urban Credit Cooperatives | 5,229 | 214.8 | |
| Trust and investment companies | 391 | n.a. | |
| People's Insurance Company of China | 5,240 | 66.1 | |
| China Pacific Insurance Company | n.a. | 4.2 | |
| Finance companies | 29 | 27.6 | |
| Financial leasing companies | 11 | n.a. | |
| Securities companies | 87 | n.a. | |
| Mutual fund companies | 43 | n.a. | |

| Foreign financial institutions (representatives' offices) | | |
| --- | --- | --- |
| Foreign banks | 250 | n.a. |
| Foreign finance companies | 4 | n.a. |
| Foreign investment companies | 7 | n.a. |
| Foreign insurance companies | 70 | n.a. |
| Foreign securities companies | 40 | n.a. |
| Foreign credit card companies | 4 | n.a. |
| Other | 18 | n.a. |

- 1994: Budget Law passed by the National People's Congress prohibiting government borrowing from the Central Bank. Establishment of State Development Bank; Export–Import Bank; Agricultural Development Bank.

- 1995: Adoption of the Law on the People's Bank of China and the Commercial Banking Law.

- January 1996: Establishment of national interbank market with liberalized interest rates. Announcement that open market operations will commence from April 1, 1996.

*Sources:* World Bank, *The Chinese Economy: Fighting Inflation, Deepening Reforms* (Washington, DC: The World Bank, 1996), 26; People's Bank of China, *China's Financial Outlook,* 1995; *China Statistical Yearbook,* 1995; *Almanac of China's Finance and Banking,* 1995.
— is none.
n.a. is not available.
*Note:* Data are for 1994.

industrial ministries also play prominent roles in setting trade policy and industrial policy in their sectors.

## The Succession Struggle

Undoubtedly, the most important political issue regarding China is that of the struggle for power now that China's paramount leader Deng Xiaoping has passed from the scene. Deng, who died on February 19, 1997, was 92 and said to be in poor health; rumors of his imminent death had circulated for years.

China's long tradition of being ruled by a strong leader dates back for centuries. Surprisingly, the advent of communism has not erased the legacy of the strong leader. Beginning with Mao Zedong, or Chairman Mao, the Chinese communist system has been dominated by a single powerful charismatic figure. Deng Xiaoping was the latest of these powerful leaders.

Deng, however, seemed uncomfortable with the tradition of vesting power in one man as opposed to institutions. He spoke against the Chinese tradition of the strong leader and gave more power to institutions; he also hand-picked a predecessor in hopes of avoiding a debilitating struggle for power. Jiang Zemin is the chosen successor.[10]

Deng is credited with engineering the rise of his protégé Jiang Zemin to the leading posts in the Chinese government. In 1992, another Deng protégé, Yang Shangkun, then the president, attempted to sweep aside Jiang, apparently because he was not seen as a sufficiently strong leader.[11] At the time, many elements of the Chinese government were willing to allow Jiang to retain at least the titles of power because he was thought to be an easy figure to push aside once Deng finally passed away.[12]

### Scenarios for Succession

Because Jiang was initially seen as such a weak leader and there were some questions regarding the stability of China after the Tiananmen Square crisis in 1989, the topic of Chinese succession was one of considerable speculation in China and around the world. Four scenarios for succession were widely discussed.

First, some attention was given to the possibility of a military takeover, perhaps to forestall a collapse of the central government. As noted, however, modern China has no history of the military directly leading China. More frequently, the military plays a role as king maker, providing key support in return for certain policy and appointment concessions.

Second, some believed that Tiananmen Square provided evidence of a popular democratic revolution, like that in the Soviet Union, shaping up in China.[13] Subsequent events, however, do not point to such a radical development. There is no evidence of a widespread democracy movement. Given the rising living standards made possible by economic growth, the populace seems fairly content. The protest at Tiananmen was led by students; it is not clear that it had the support of the general population. Especially given the military's ability and likely interest in suppressing such a movement, a democratic revolution does not appear in the immediate offing.

Many have also suggested that China might simply break apart. Proponents of this view note the increasing power of provincial governments and the increasing disparities between regions as evidence that China might simply collapse into a number of separate states.[14] Again, the PLA would seem to provide a significant impediment to such a development. Other China observers note that, although there are regional tensions within China, there is also a long tradition of one China and a high degree of homogeneity despite the presence of some vocal minorities.[15]

Finally, some have suggested that the current leading group with Jiang Zemin at the head will be able to maintain power. Some proponents of this view argue that a coalition government with several strongmen, as opposed to one, could eventually emerge. This view seems quite credible, given Jiang's apparent willingness to share power on some issues with other Chinese leaders, like Li Peng.[16]

In the early 1990s, there was no clear consensus among these views. Three years ago, a group of China experts brought together by the U.S. Defense Department to make predictions about the future course of China assigned almost equal probability to China breaking apart, undergoing a democratic revolution, or continuing to be led by a coalition of current leaders.[17]

*Recent Events*

As the Fifteenth Party Congress approaches, there is still no clear outcome to the succession struggle. Jiang retains the top leadership posts, but his potential rivals Li Peng and Qiao Shi also retain senior posts. The tensions over Taiwan in the summer of 1996 established that Jiang Zemin was still willing to allow the military to play a prominent role in setting policy on the issue that is most important to it.[18]

Jiang has also established a reputation as a consensus builder without rabid views. He has continued to move China on a course toward economic reform while accommodating those, like Li Peng, who hold more conservative views.[19]

In addition to holding all of the titles of power, Jiang has also been able to bring a number of his key supporters onto the Politburo and its Standing Committee. Though there are still recent reports of others, notably Qiao Shi, making moves that some consider to be efforts to displace Jiang, these efforts have yet to bear fruit.[20] There are also reports of Jiang seeking to add the exalted title of chairman to his list of titles, a title first held by Mao Zedong and vacant for some time. Still other reports suggest that Li Peng and Qiao Shi may be under pressure to accept "brightly lit shelf" positions and move off of the Politburo's Standing Committee.[21] At this point, all of these views are essentially based upon rumor, but there does seem to be an increasingly credible view that Deng's long, slow decline has allowed Jiang to consolidate power.

*Is the Succession Struggle Over?*

It may, in fact, be that the succession struggle is over. Deng was in such poor health for years that he was likely incapable of participating in governing decisions. Day-to-day decisions have undoubtedly been made for some years now by Jiang and his ruling coalition. The military seems comfortable with Jiang. There are continuing tensions between the regions, but there is no evidence to suggest that they are building toward a breakaway, particularly if there is no crisis in Beijing. More interestingly, some of China's dissidents in exile recently published a widely read essay arguing that the time for violent revolution in China had passed and that it was better to work for evolutionary change.

History would indicate that totalitarian and authoritarian regimes can never be said to be truly stable. There are almost always dissatisfied elements that can sometimes pull together into a rebellion with remarkable speed, a la the Soviet Union. Certainly, a country with a history of violent revolution, like China, would always seem vulnerable to sudden, unpredictable political upheaval. This reality must be kept in mind in any assessment of the future prospects of the current regime in a post-Deng era.

All that said, however, the current regime led by Jiang seems to have a firm hold on power and to be relatively stable. Since this regime seems to be more rule by an inclusive coalition in which most factions have a voice than rule by a single strong leader, future power struggles seem likely to be fought over particular policy issues, not over the hold on power of the current group of leaders. This would seem to indicate that continued reform is possible but that sudden dramatic change is unlikely.

On the economic front, Jiang is seen as a supporter of reform. Deng's son recently delivered a speech criticizing the current group of leaders for backing away from the cause of reform and damaging Deng's legacy.[22] This seems somewhat of an overstatement. Economic reform has slowed, and communist institutions, such as the State Planning Agency and SOEs, have reasserted themselves. There seems, however, to be no major group advocating a radical departure from the fundamental pillars of Deng's economic reforms—foreign investment and exports. In short, left to its own devices, further progress in China on economic policy is likely to be slow, but abandonment of Deng's basic policies is unlikely. As one Chinese scholar remarked to the author on a recent visit: "No one, not even the generals, can afford to abandon reform."

This means that the current regime is likely to retain control of China for the foreseeable future. Thus, the economic problems inherent in integrating China into the world economy are unlikely to change dramatically on their own. If anything, the continued growth of the Chinese economy, the growth of Chinese exports, and the continued influx of investment will likely make the current problems larger. Instead of waiting for internal reform that is unlikely to come, the rest of the world should now focus on the economic challenges posed by China's emergence as an economic power and develop a concrete strategy for addressing them.

## Notes

1. For a good discussion of modern Chinese politics, see Harry Harding, *A Fragile Relationship: The United States and China since 1972* (Washington, DC: The Brookings Institution, 1992).

2. "What Next for China?" *Economist,* October 22, 1994, 37–38.

3. Tony Walker, "Chinese Rivals Use Western Press to Air Differences," *Financial Times,* September 11, 1996.

4. Ibid.

5. *Managing the Taiwan Issue: Key Is Better U.S. Relations with China,* Report of an Independent Task Force, (New York: Council on Foreign Relations, 1995).

6. Harry Harding, *A Fragile Relationship,* 1992, 216–23.

7. Kathy Chen, "Soldiers of Fortune: Chinese Army Fashions Major Role for Itself as a Business Empire," *Wall Street Journal,* May 24, 1994.

8. United States Trade Representative, *1996 National Trade Estimate Report on Foreign Trade Barriers* (Washington, DC: USTR, 1996), 50.

9. Ibid., 46.

10. Stephen Mufson, "Chinese Party Tries to Please All Sides," *International Herald Tribune,* October 12, 1996.

11. Willy Wo-Lap Lam, "Yang Throws Down Gauntlet," *South China Morning Post,* July 21, 1996; and "Among the Hopefuls, Ho Jintao Stands the Best Chance as China's Next Supremo," *Straits Times,* September 25, 1996, 8.

12. Ian Johnson, "Five Men Maneuver To Rule China," *Sun* (Baltimore), February 5, 1995; and Patrick Tyler, "In China, Politicians Prepare for the Post-Deng Era," *New York Times,* August 30, 1996, A11.

13. Michael D. Swaine, *China—Domestic Change and Foreign Policy* (Santa Monica, CA: RAND, 1995).

14. Ibid.

15. Ronald Morse, "Broken China?" *International Economy* (January/February 1995), 30–32.

16. Yasheng Huang, "Why China Will Not Collapse," *Foreign Policy,* June 22, 1995, 54.

17. Ronald Morse, "Broken China?" 30–32.

18. Willy Wo-Lap Lam, "Army Seeks Bigger Say in Foreign Policy; Use of Force 'Must be an Option against Taiwan,' " *South China Morning Post,* August 1, 1996.

19. Joyce Barnathan, with Stan Crock and Bruce Einhorn, "Rethinking China," *Business Week,* March 4, 1996.

20. Willy Wo-Lap Lam, "Qiao's Bid for the Throne," *South China Morning Post,* April 3, 1996, 21.

21. Patrick E. Tyler, "China's Ambitious President Wants Mao's Title: Chairman," *New York Times,* August 20, 1996; and Rod Mickleburgh, "Man Who Changed China Just Fading Away," *The Globe and Mail,* August 22, 1996, 7.

22. Anthoney Spaeth, Jaime Florcruz, and Mia Turner, "The Deng Fadeout," *Time,* October 7, 1996.

# Part II

## Barriers to Integration

In the modern world, no economy can be classified as purely communist or purely capitalist. All fall at some point on a continuum between the two extremes; none puts all its faith in the market and none puts all its faith in state planning. In a discussion of the problems raised by integrating China into the world economy, however, two important observations can be made with regard to the placement of countries on this continuum.

First, even before the fall of the Soviet Union, countries were moving away from the communist pole. Today, even the die-hard advocates of communism are making reforms. Cuba has begun to experiment with private enterprise on a small scale.[1] An increasingly desperate North Korea is setting up free enterprise zones similar to the SEZs established by China.[2] Vietnam has already gone much further and is following a path of development through reform very similar to China's.[3] In fact, although Vietnam and China have strong political differences, China seems to have created the model Vietnam is now eagerly following. No economy in the world currently strives to practice communism in its pure form, and market reform has gained near-universal support in principle, if not in practice.

Second, before it began the current round of market reforms, China was one of the countries that maintained an economy close to the communist end of the spectrum. The state's power over the economy and most other aspects of life was nearly absolute. Workers could not change jobs without government permission. The state was able to implement economic plans that now seem ridiculous, such as wiping out sparrows because they ate grain or turning every village into a steel producer. As absurd as these plans were, they were pursued with gusto and achieved considerable "success" in their dubious objectives. For example, the population of sparrows was dramatically reduced by Mao Zedong's efforts. Unfortunately, this resulted in a population explosion of insects that were formerly eaten by the birds, which actually resulted in more grain losses and, ultimately, famine. This incident should spark new respect for the natural ecology and the can-do attitude of the Chinese people. It is also a chilling demonstration of the raw power wielded by the government.[4]

China has made considerable progress in moving toward the market end of the continuum, but it still has far to go. It remains one of the few formally communist systems in the world. Given the change that has taken place and continues to take place in China, there is a temptation to dismiss that commitment as merely rhetorical. This would be a mistake. Economic, political, and cultural remnants of communism remain throughout the Chinese system and pose significant barriers to China's shouldering a full-fledged role in the world economy and its key institutions. Even in those areas where China is actively attempting to shed the holdovers from the old system, its new institutions are often not fully in place. Part II reviews the challenges that must be confronted in order to bring China into the world market economy, including remnants of the totalitarian system, traditional trade barriers, the lack of an established rule of law, and the foreign exchange management system employed by China. Each of these issues will be analyzed separately, but it is important to appreciate that, in most respects, they are very closely linked, perhaps even different symptoms of the same problem.

## Notes

1. Howard La Franchi, "Free Enterprise Gains in Communist Cuba," *Christian Science Monitor,* April 4, 1996.

2. Sang-Hun Choe, "North Korea Seeks Outside Cash to Save Economy," *Associated Press,* October 6, 1995.

3. "A Difficult Time to Be a Vietnamese Communist," *Economist,* June 8, 1996.

4. For a discussion of the history of these events see Jonathan D. Spence, *The Search for Modern China* (New York: W.W. Norton, 1990).

# 4

# The Totalitarian System

Perhaps because economic, political, and cultural issues are so often discussed separately, there is a tendency to consider them as independent issues. This is simply untrue. As experience with Japan has demonstrated, even after formal trade barriers have been dismantled, free trade is very difficult to achieve with a country that has a cultural resistance of imports and foreign influence.[1] Similarly, a brief review of the political environment in countries around the world reveals that democracy and respect for human rights are often associated with a degree of economic prosperity.[2] In the case of China, the totalitarian political system has had lasting economic impact.

For example, to even engage in foreign commerce—that is, importing or exporting—firms and individuals in China must obtain government permission.[3] The process for obtaining this permission, referred to as trading rights, has been streamlined somewhat in recent years. Many observers familiar with Chinese practices contend that the problems in obtaining trading rights normally have more to do with corruption or parochialism in the relevant ministries than a government policy of protection. Nonetheless, government control of all trading rights continues to exist.

Elimination of trading rights has been the topic of recent international negotiations aimed at China's membership in the WTO. China has tabled proposals to address trading rights, but the operational details are unclear. Under the Chinese proposal it is clear, however, that even if some sort of automatic trading right is granted to foreign-owned enterprises, no similar automatic right would be extended to Chinese-owned businesses and Chinese citizens.

With further negotiation, the status of the trading rights may change, but the issue is symptomatic of a larger problem. At this point, the Chinese government's control of economic activities is so extensive as to make normal commerce impossible. Current trade negotiations with China focus on traditional issues, such as tariffs and quotas, but as long as the Chinese government maintains control of all trading rights, these negotiations have an air of unreality about them. With trading rights limitations in place, the Chinese government can control all imports and exports. Even if it were to unilaterally renounce all other trade barriers, it would be possible for China to block all imports by withholding trading rights.

Unless the Chinese government is willing to permanently relinquish direct control of economic activities, nothing approaching free trade is possible with China. Rumors have recently circulated suggesting that Beijing was contemplating major reforms on trading rights and other issues. Experience would indicate, however, that the eventual reality rarely lives up to the rumor.[4] Further, Chinese officials have restated publicly that they are still not prepared to take such steps and remain deeply suspicious of the market as an organizing mechanism. This small example exposes the problem that China's totalitarian system poses to economic integration.

### State-Owned Enterprises

The most obvious holdover of the communist era in China is its more than 100,000 state-owned enterprises (SOEs). These enterprises range from large manufacturing operations with thousands of employees to small local ventures with only a few. The largest are concentrated in "heavy" manufacturing, such as steel and chemicals.[5]

Most of the SOEs, particularly the larger ones, have intimate ties with the government agencies responsible for their sectors. For example, the Ministry of the Chemical Industry operates a number of chemical plants; the Ministry of the Electronics Industry electrical facilities, and so on. This intimate relationship results in some trade complications. Often a ministry that operates firms in a particular industry also decides if imports are permitted in that sector.[6] Not surprisingly, the ministries are generally not enthusiastic about imports. Similar problems result in industries heavily dependent upon intellectual property. In the chemical sector, for example, the Ministry of the Chemical Industry has insisted upon examining formulas for imported agricultural chemicals as well as samples. Often, similar or identical chemicals are soon produced by a ministry-owned facility.[7]

Reform of the SOEs has been a topic in China for a number of years. As market reform has progressed, the task has become increasingly urgent, as it has become apparent that most of the state industries are operating in the red and, in many cases, deeply so. The stories surrounding China's efforts at reforming the SOEs are in some ways typical of those experienced by all communist countries that attempt economic reform. Chinese officials tell of managers unfamiliar with the basic accounting practices needed to determine if the enterprise is making a profit or incurring a loss, and of managers unable to come to grips with the concept of paying back government "loans" after years of receiving state aid.[8]

A number of reforms have been attempted, all of which have the general goal of making the SOEs more market-based enterprises. These include changing the makeup of the governing board, privatizing competitive SOEs, and allowing the SOEs that simply are not salvageable to declare bankruptcy. Unfortunately, China has been ill prepared to deal with the costs of these policies, most notably unemployment. By some estimates, reform of the state industries has already put millions of Chinese out of work, and more than 110 million Chinese are still employed by SOEs.[9] Many of these workers are still paid by the state, but unemployment appears to have become a significant source of unrest in some regions. Since in the communist system all workers were automatically assigned jobs, the problem of unemployed workers, some of whom lack employable skills, is a difficulty that China has not yet developed the infrastructure to confront.

As a result of these problems, the pace of state industry reform has been, at best, uneven. Recently the Chinese government has extended some special low-interest loans to troubled SOEs to avoid further unemployment. Judging from the comments of Chinese political leaders, there is considerable concern over the political cost of continued reform. In fact, in 1996, state lending to SOEs actually increased by 100 billion yuan ($12 billion).[10] This would seem to indicate that the SOE sector is unlikely to shrink dramatically in the near future.

All observers of China's SOEs agree on two points. First, due to reforms, the percentage of China's economy tied to SOEs is shrinking. Second, the nonstate sector is growing more rapidly than the state sector. The actual size of the SOEs, however, is subject to some debate. A recent World Bank review held that SOEs' share of China's GDP had shrunk from 60 percent to about 31 percent; some observers believe the SOEs' share of GDP will soon shrink even further.[11] Earlier studies have put the size of the SOE sector at closer to 50 percent, with collectives making up 40 percent of GDP, and truly individually owned enterprises comprising only about 10 percent.[12] Of course, given that the size of China's GDP is also subject to substantial debate, these figures cannot be regarded as certain; if the size of the economy is unknown it is, of course, impossible to calculate the share held by SOEs.

Beyond that, several other problems make it difficult to define the state industry sector. First, the category of collective is a very broad one. It includes some companies that are merely subsidiaries of SOEs, some enterprises of local government, and some that might truly be called private sector enterprises. In addition, the dividing line between government and private sector enterprises is not clear.[13] For example, many central and provincial government officials and their families have direct ties to business ventures. The business interests of Chinese government officials have posed problems for U.S. efforts to address both piracy of intellectual property and arms sales; Chinese government officials have been loathe to take actions that would hurt earnings of the companies involved in these transactions because of their personal interest in the companies.[14]

Second, many ostensibly private companies have other financial ties to the government, such as having relied on government loans to begin operations. Finally, even estimates by international financial institutions or other disinterested parties rely heavily on data from official Chinese sources, which are open to debate.

In any event, no one could disagree that SOEs are still responsible for a substantial share of China's GDP, but the government's control of the economy goes far beyond those enterprises it directly owns. State-issued economic plans set policy on all ventures, including private and foreign-owned ones.

## Economic Planning

Since the communist takeover of China, the state planning apparatus has run the economy through an unbroken string of five-year economic plans, the ninth and latest of which was issued in the fall of 1995. These plans do not include specific details on the operation of all aspects of the economy; much of that is left to policies tailored by the ministries and the marketplace. They do, however, provide a broad outline for government economic policy and indicate the direction of policy changes in the coming five years.[15] As has often been the case in recent years, statements in the latest plan indicated some tension between economic reformers and those who would prefer to continue traditional Chinese economic policy. It did appear, however, that enthusiasm for reform in state industries has lagged.[16]

Perhaps the most notable feature of these plans is their continued existence. Five-year economic plans are the hallmark of the communist economic system. The continuing existence of a government planning structure does indicate an unwillingness to rely upon the market to make resource allocation and other economic decisions. This is to take nothing away from the real and substantial economic reforms China has carried out, particularly with regard to market enterprises in the coastal provinces. It is important to keep in mind, however, that the stated goal of present reforms in planning documents is not to move to an entirely capitalist system. Economic plans and political leaders used terms, like *market-based socialism,* to describe the ideal economic system. For example, Chinese Premier Li Peng was recently quoted as saying, "The socialist system is worthy of being the right choice of the Chinese people. . . . We must ceaselessly push forward . . . the building of modern socialism. . . ."[17]

The sectoral economic plans issued by Chinese ministries pose a more serious barrier to China's economic integration into the world system. China has long maintained plans to promote "pillar industries," including but not limited to automobiles, electronics, and machinery.[18] In recent years, the Chinese government has issued new plans for the automobile and pharmaceutical industries and announced that further plans would be forthcoming.[19] A plan is also rumored to be pending and perhaps even to be completed for the electronics industry.[20] Disturbingly, reports in the Chinese press hold that a number of Chinese ministries are drafting industrial policies "modeled after those of Japan and South Korea."[21] On the same topic, the office of the U.S. Trade Representative (USTR) noted that the original pillar industry plans are not being abandoned outright, but rather replaced with new industrial plans.[22]

The trade and economic problems caused by Chinese policies go beyond those sectors in which explicit plans are in place. For example, Chinese officials stridently point out that China has no formal aerospace plan, yet the government is clearly attempting to nurture an aerospace industry. Chinese publications have for years touted the goal of building a "people's airplane," and negotiations have been under way to launch such a venture with the possible assistance of South Korea and a western airplane manufacturer.[23]

China is an enormous present and future market for airliners—a market that none of the three major airliner manufacturers can afford to ignore. As a result, the Boeing Company, McDonnell Douglas Corporation, and Airbus Industries have all been aggressively seeking a role in the Chinese market. As a quid pro quo for aircraft purchases China has insisted that some of the manufacturing of the aircraft occur in China and that, as a result, technology and know-how associated with commercial aircraft manufacturing be transferred to China.[24]

The aircraft companies have all complied with the request. McDonnell Douglas assembles MD-80 and MD-90 passenger jets in Shanghai and builds aircraft nose cones in Chengdu. Boeing makes parts of both the 737 and 747 in Xian, parts of the 757 in Chengdu, 757 cargo doors in Shenyang, and 737 components in Shanghai. Airbus has been a late entrant, but now produces parts for the A300, A310, A320, and A340 in Xian and Shenyang. Airbus has also been working to expand relationships in China, which could lead to a greater transfer of production and technology.[25]

Drawing a rather fine distinction, Chinese government officials will insist that this is not the result of an industry plan of the type announced in the automotive sector. This statement is true as far as it goes, but it does not mean that the above-noted decisions are not the result of government policy. It is difficult to believe that Boeing felt the market dictated that tail sections for 737s are best assembled in Xian and then shipped back to Seattle for assembly into the completed aircraft. Similar arguments could be made in each of the cases listed. As Chinese officials have noted, the price of selling aircraft to China is transfer of production and technology. Whether it is called an industrial policy or merely a policy on foreign investment, it has the same effect. In numerous sectors, like large civilian aircraft, informal policies operate that are in all meaningful respects industrial policies.

As noted in the previous section, Chinese exports are increasingly composed of higher-value manufactured products. As the office of the USTR noted: "China's growing focus on certain 'pillar industries'—including machinery, electronics, and autos among others—is becoming increasingly evident in the composition of China's trade."[26] If the pattern set by Japan and Korea is followed, this pattern can be expected to accelerate as these policies continue to operate.

Far from being innocuous guidelines, the recently released plans explicitly violate not only the WTO but also bilateral trade agreements with the United States. Provisions aimed at import substitution, not importing products for which a domestically produced replacement is available, are included in both plans. Those in the automotive plan directly violate the provisions of a 1992 agreement between China and the United States in which China agreed to end all import substitution policies. In effect, the auto plan also imposes increasing domestic content requirements on foreign-owned auto manufacturers operating in China; government criticism of foreign auto companies for using too many imported auto parts in the automobiles they assemble in China indicate that the plan is being implemented.[27] Press reports indicate the electronics plan contains similar WTO-inconsistent provisions.[28] The technology transfer requirements imposed on large civilian aircraft and other imported manufacturing products also appear to violate both the 1992 bilateral agreement and the WTO.[29]

Plans and other directives of Chinese ministries also frequently include two other policy devices that are often inconsistent with trade agreements and always inconsistent with the principles of free trade: trade or foreign exchange balancing requirements and various performance requirements on foreign investments. Trade balancing provisions require firms operating in China, usually foreign joint ventures, to export as much as they import or, more frequently, more than they import. This ensures that foreign ventures will make a positive contribution to China's trade balance.[30]

Performance requirements are closely related; in fact, broadly speaking, trade balancing requirements are one type of performance requirement. Simply put, performance requirements are measures required as a condition for investing in China. One of the most frequently imposed requirements is that a certain percentage of production must be exported.[31] Foreign joint ventures often face very high export performance requirements— sometimes as high as 100 percent. Another typical performance requirement involves transfer of technology. Both the United States and Europe have pressed China to curb these requirements in WTO accession negotiations.

## Imitating Japan and Korea?

If China's plans are truly based upon those of Japan and South Korea, which surely seems to be the case, further trade problems are virtually inevitable. There is a long history of conflict between the United States, on the one side, and Japan and South Korea, on the other, over industries that were the target of industrial policy, including steel, automobiles, and semiconductors.[32] Similar difficulties are already arising in the sectors China is focusing its attention upon. From the perspective of the industrial policymakers in Japan and South Korea, industrial policies have been successful.[33] Domestic industries were built up and exports of the targeted products have surged. Both Japan and South Korea are now leading players in the targeted industry.

The perceived success of these industrial plans is one of the reasons they are likely attractive to the Chinese. Unfortunately, these industrial policies were quite costly to other countries, which lost jobs and manufacturing facilities as a result of the exports and increased production the policies created. In short, if past experience is any guide, there is ample reason for the rest of the world to be very concerned with China's industrial policies.

## State Power

The power of Chinese ministries to regulate economic activity goes beyond formal economic and industrial plans. For example, rather than let demand for imports be determined by market forces, as is the case in true market economies, Chinese ministries determine demand themselves. The State Planning Agency (SPA), the State Economic and Trade Commission (SETC), and the Ministry of Foreign Trade and Economic Coordination (MOFTEC) jointly set import "demand." Quotas, import licenses, and other import controls are then employed to ensure that the actual level of imports does not exceed "demand." As will be discussed in more detail in the next chapter, this process, like many others, is not transparent; the formula used to determine "demand" is a mystery. Obviously, there is enormous potential for these "behind closed doors" decisions to result in protectionism and discrimination against foreign companies or even against a particular foreign company.[34]

Unfortunately, the process of setting import "demand" is typical of other ministry decisions on economic and regulatory matters. Ministries have considerable influence over matters ranging from citing operations to hiring of local staff. Often these decisions are made without transparent procedures and without leaving any "paper trail" to be second-guessed. This makes it easy to quietly retaliate against a particular country or a particular company. It is difficult to police this kind of discrimination through traditional international dispute settlement procedures; without a "paper trail" it is very difficult to prove discrimination.

**Nationalism and Free Trade**

Even more difficult to address than the quiet discrimination of particular ministries is the problem created by nationalism or antiforeign sentiments. Though a full discussion is beyond the scope of this book, much of Japan's continuing protectionism is attributed to a cultural distrust of those companies and products that are not Japanese. Chinese culture and history are different from those of Japan, but there are rising antiforeign, antiwestern, and particularly anti–United States sentiments in China.

A recent anti–United States book entitled *China Can Say No* is now very popular in China. It is modeled on a similar book entitled *Japan Can Say No,* which urged Japan to adopt a more aggressive strategy in refusing U.S. trade demands. The Chinese version is written by young Chinese intellectuals and makes a number of stridently antiwestern sentiments with a chapter entitled "Why I Will Never Fly on a Boeing Airplane," which urges avoiding U.S.-made products in retaliation for western attitudes toward China.[35] Various campaigns against imports and products with western-sounding names have also emerged.[36] The state-run press continually pounds away at the United States and other western countries. For example, during the 1996 summer Olympics the state press accused western countries of a conspiracy to deny China gold medals in gymnastics and softball. NBC, the U.S. network covering the Olympics, was also accused of attempting to make the Chinese volleyball team appear shorter than the American team.[37]

These anti-U.S. statements may appear trivial or even humorous, but in a country with memories of Tiananmen Square and the Cultural Revolution, the average Chinese citizen must take notice of government sentiments. Further, without any outside information to counter the propaganda, much of the government sentiment is probably taken to heart. For example, it is reported that Chinese schoolchildren often divide into teams in order to play games in which the "good guys" are Chinese and the "bad guys" are Americans.

With anti-American and antiwestern sentiments running so high and aggressively fanned by the government, it will likely be difficult for American companies to establish normal commercial relationships and will certainly be difficult to market American brand-name consumer products in China. Unfortunately, since this problem is so intimately tied into political tensions and national rivalries, it is very difficult to address and is certainly beyond the scope of any trade arrangement.

### Conclusion

It is not impossible for the United States to establish a trading relationship with countries that are authoritarian or totalitarian, but there is a connection between political and personal freedom and the free marketplace. The very notion that economic and industrial plans should guide certain decisions is incompatible with the free market system; market economics holds that these decisions are made by the marketplace not by governments. Clearly, the trade barriers included in Chinese economic plans directly violate international trade agreements.

Beyond these economic plans, totalitarian governments, like China, are able to exert enormous influence over economic activity. No enterprise can operate without the approval, or at least tolerance, of the government. If firms and individuals fear government disapproval or censure for doing business with foreign companies, it is an obvious direct infringement in commerce.

Therefore, as China seeks further economic integration with the world economy, particularly through increased trade, it is impossible to ignore the Chinese political system. This issue is of particular relevance to China's efforts to join the WTO. The WTO can be effective in policing formal trade barriers or direct governmental action, but it is utterly incapable of policing decisions reached behind closed doors and quietly implemented. In the case of China, it may often be impossible to prove that action has even been taken against foreign governments or companies. Thus, the idea of policing these decisions through a distant dispute settlement body is nearly laughable.

In short, there is a connection between the free marketplace of ideas and the free marketplace. If China wishes true economic integration with the world, it must be prepared to limit governmental authority to meddle in private affairs and economic activity. At a bare minimum, all governmental decisions on foreign companies and imports must be made public and be consistent with international agreements. The process for enforcing them must also be transparent. Only China can determine if it is willing to undertake this level of political reform. For their part, western countries, particularly the United States, must carefully consider whether a country given to indoctrinating its citizens with antiwestern rhetoric will make a good trading partner.

# Notes

1. Chalmers Johnson, *Japan: Who Governs?* (New York: W.W. Norton, 1995).

2. Bryan T. Johnson and Thomas P. Sheehy, *1996 Index of Economic Freedom* (Washington, DC: The Heritage Foundation, 1996).

3. See Clinton administration trading rights paper; for published discussion Greg Mastel, "Beijing at Bay," *Foreign Policy* (fall 1996), 29.

4. Martin Crutsinger, "China Trade Offers Please U.S.," Associated Press, February 12, 1997.

5. World Bank, *The Chinese Economy: Fighting Inflation, Deepening Reforms*, A World Bank Country Study (Washington, DC: The World Bank, 1996), 15–21; and Matt Forney, "Trial by Fire," *Far East Economic Review*, September 12, 1996, 62–68.

6. United States Trade Representative (hereafter USTR), *1996 National Trade Estimate Report on Foreign Trade Barriers* (Washington, DC: USTR, 1996), 47.

7. U.S.-China Business Council, "Chemical Companies Oppose Registration Requirements," press release, September 20, 1994.

8. Matt Forney, "Trial by Fire," 62–68.

9. Ibid., and World Bank, *The Chinese Economy*, 15–24.

10. Renee Schoof, "Beijing Financial," *AP Online*, July 15, 1996.

11. World Bank, *The Chinese Economy*, 16.

12. World Bank, *China: Reform of State Owned Enterprises* (Washington, DC: The World Bank, 1995).

13. World Bank, *Bureaucrats in Business: The Economics and Politics of Government Ownership* (New York: Oxford University Press, 1995), 66.

14. Lu Ning, "Teaming Up China's PLA May Pay Off: Analyst" *BT Online*, November 15, 1996; and "China 'Princeling' Charged with Graft," *BT Online*, October 19, 1996.

15. "Chinese Officials Study 5-Year Economic Plan," *Asian Economic News*, December 11, 1995.

16. Simon Holberton, "China to Back New Five-Year Plan," *Financial Times*, September 26, 1995.

17. Benjamin Kang Lim, "Socialism Right Choice For China—Premier Li Peng," *Reuters World Service*, July 29, 1996.

18. USTR, *1996 National Trade Estimate*, 50.

19. Ibid.

20. Ibid.

21. Lu Ning, "The Cost of Nationalism," *Business Times*, July 25, 1996; and "Japan's New Identity," *Business Week*, April 10, 1995.

22. USTR, *1996 National Trade Estimate*, 46.

23. Stanley Holmes, "How Boeing Woos Beijing," *Seattle Times*, May 26, 1996.

24. Greg Mastel, "The Art of the Steal," *Washington Post*, February 19, 1994.

25. Holmes, "How Boeing Woos Beijing"; and Lewis M. Simons, "High Tech Jobs For Sale," *Time*, July 22, 1996.

26. USTR, *1996 National Trade Estimate*, 46.

27. "How the Mighty Have Fallen in China," *EIU Business China*, April 29, 1996.

28. USTR, *1996 National Trade Estimate*, 50.

29. *Memorandum of Understanding Between the Government of the United States of America and the Government of the People's Republic of China, Concerning Market Access*, 1992, Article II 1(iv).

30. USTR, *1996 National Trade Estimate*, 57.

31. Ibid.

32. Johnson, *Japan: Who Governs?* and Danny M. Leipziger and Peter Petri, *Korean Industrial Policy*, a World Bank discussion paper (Washington, DC: The World Bank, 1993).

33. Ibid.

34. USTR, *1996 National Trade Estimate*, 47.

35. Benjamin Kang Lim, "China in Love–Hate Relationship With U.S.," *Reuters World Service*, November 17, 1996.

36. Steven Mufson, "China's Shaky Grip; a Nation of Contradictions Gropes for an Identity," *Washington Post*, November 17, 1996.

37. Steven Mufson, "China Puts Forth Persistent, Caustic Anti-U.S. Themes; Diversity of Complaints Hints at Reservoir of Grievances," *Washington Post*, August 12, 1996; Ian Johnson, "China Is Claiming Conspiracy; Country's Official Line Has Its Athletes Being Cheated Out of Gold," *Baltimore Sun*, August 1, 1996; and, "Masterkova Sets World Mark in Her First 1–Mile Competition," *Sun Sentinel* (Fort Lauderdale), August 15, 1996.

# 5

# Rule of Law

One of China's brightest political rising stars, if men of seventy years can be known as rising stars, is Qiao Shi. Currently, he is chairman of the National People's Congress (NPC). Under his leadership, the NPC has evolved from a simple rubber-stamp body into something approaching a more traditional legislature. Although it has not yet overturned any of the leadership decisions of either the Communist Party or the government, there has been significant opposition to the appointment of certain officials and to the government's infamous Three Gorges dam project.[1] This opposition sounds fairly tame from the perspective of western democracies, but in China it is a sign of some tolerance of dissent and of the NPC's admittedly limited efforts to gain a voice in a totalitarian society.

Qiao hardly has the background of a democracy advocate. Much of his career was spent in China's internal security forces, which control dissent using sometimes brutal means. He has, however, become one of the most prominent possible alternatives to China's current leader, Jiang Zemin. Last year, for example, he undertook a high-profile international tour with stops in Russia, Cuba, Ukraine, and Canada.[2]

Perhaps the most interesting facet of Qiao's recent activities is his strident advocacy of establishing a rule of law in China. It may sound odd that a country with a totalitarian government cannot enforce laws, but this is one of the central problems facing China. As Qiao puts it: "These [democratic] systems and laws must not change because of the change of leaders."[3] The distinction he makes is between a country with a strong and reliable legal system and a country ruled instead by the whims of its leaders, whims that often change with leadership changes. China has a long and unfortunate history of events, like the Cultural Revolution and the tragedy at Tiananmen Square, that demonstrate the near absolute authority of leaders. It is far from having a legal system capable of reliably bringing order and establishing legal principles immune from interference by leaders. In short, China is a country of strong leaders, not strong laws.

Qiao's campaign to establish a rule of law in China may at first seem only distantly connected to the topic of this book. Upon closer examination, however, it becomes clear that China's lack of reliable rule of law and the many problems it creates is the single largest barrier to integrating China into the world economy. Consider the following four diverse examples of problems caused by China's lack of a rule of law.

### Intellectual Property

The United States and China have been engaged in active discussions of trade and commercial problems for just over a decade. (Of course, commercial issues have been on the agenda since President Richard Nixon's trip to China, but they were clearly not on top of the agenda.) Throughout this ongoing dialogue, a leading concern for the United States has been the protection of intellectual property.[4] The United States excels in the production of intellectual property—patented, trademarked, or copyrighted material. Intellectual property products such as films, sound recordings, and computer programs consistently make a strong positive contribution to the U.S. trade balance.

Gaining protection of intellectual property is a challenge the United States and other western countries face in most poorer countries. It can be particularly difficult in countries that have operated under a communist system in which the very notion of owning an idea is foreign. In China, for example, there is an adage to the effect that stealing a book is an honorable crime.

Chinese scholars sometimes make the claim that the copying of a book written by them is a compliment, not an affront. Of course, as the notion of royalty payments becomes better understood, this sentiment seems to be changing.

Even in China, however, few would now challenge the concept of protecting intellectual property, at least in theory. Ironically, even as China has gained a better understanding of the reasons to protect intellectual property, piracy of intellectual property has grown into a multibillion-dollar industry. By the early 1990s, Chinese intellectual property pirates had become enormously successful producing, selling, and often exporting pirated material, primarily from western countries.[5] Most companies operating in China have their own stories of intellectual property piracy; the U.S. auto maker Chrysler even had knock-off artists producing illegal copies of its jeeps.[6] Most of the piracy was, however, concentrated upon products, such as agricultural chemicals, films, computer programs, and sound recordings.

After the United States threatened China with trade sanctions in 1992, the Bush administration concluded an agreement with China aimed at ending piracy of intellectual property. Under the terms of the agreement, China agreed to adopt a complete set of intellectual property laws covering patents, trademarks, and copyrights. On paper, these amendments put China's intellectual property laws on a par with those of many leading western countries. The new Chinese statutes exceeded the minimum standard set by the WTO. Then–U.S. Trade Representative Carla Hills triumphantly proclaimed that China had adopted a "world class" intellectual property law.[7]

Unfortunately, the world class laws changed little in practice. They were simply not consistently enforced. Between 1992 and 1994, piracy of intellectual property went from being a hidden cottage industry to a full-scale export industry. In southern China, dozens of factories pirated intellectual property, primarily U.S. films, recordings, and computer programs, on compact discs better known as CDs. The CDs were then often exported to markets as far away as Eastern Europe, Canada, and the western United States because China had only limited domestic demand for such products. Computer programs worth thousands of dollars could be purchased for as little as $10–$30 on the streets of Beijing. Even Chinese government ministries reportedly employed pirated computer programs.[8]

In 1993, the Clinton administration took up the challenge of combating Chinese intellectual property piracy. In February of 1994, a deal was struck with the Chinese government that focused on enforcing Chinese laws. Unfortunately, this agreement also failed to stem the tide of Chinese piracy. One year after the agreement, China had made some efforts to crack down on piracy. The primary effect was to put some street-level dealers out of business. The factories, however, continued to operate. In fact, new factories had opened and pirated goods production had actually risen. Further, China simply refused to implement important provisions of the 1994 agreement. After the threat of imposing about $2 billion in trade sanctions on China, the United States and China reached a third understanding on intellectual property in the summer of 1996.[9] As this is written, it is too early to judge the effect of this new meeting of the minds on intellectual property. As the current USTR Charlene Barshefsky has said, however, convincing China to end intellectual property piracy will be a "long process."[10]

The intellectual property piracy problem illustrates the difficulty of attempting to establish a normal commercial relationship with a country without a rule of law. Obviously, international agreements and changes in Chinese law have not been enough to actually alter Chinese behavior. In fact, the most important lesson of the intellectual property experience is that these formal, legal changes have been virtually worthless. The western assumption that a change in the laws will bring about changes in behavior has proven totally false in China. Even more interesting is the reason that Chinese officials gave for the failure of previous agreements to halt piracy. One frequently advanced explanation is that Chinese provincial governments, relatives of leading central government officials (often referred to as "princelings"), and elements of the central government, most notably the PLA, were all directly involved in the piracy. Prominent princelings were known to own interests in the pirate companies. The PLA also owned an interest in some of the factories and, in at least one instance, allowed a factory to operate on the grounds of a PLA facility.[11] Given this array of forces and the cooling in U.S.-China relations, officials intimated that the central government simply would not and perhaps could not enforce the agreement.

## Sales of Nuclear Materials

Another frequent issue in U.S.-China diplomacy has been China's sale of dangerous weapons and technology potentially useful in the production of nuclear weapons to dangerous countries, such as Iran and Pakistan. China has been implicated in the sale of cruise missile technology and nuclear reactors to Iran,[12] although China contends that reactors were sold only after internationally accepted safeguard measures were taken.[13] To Pakistan, China has sold missiles capable of delivering a nuclear payload,[14] and, most recently, technology used in the production of nuclear weapons.[15]

These sales are interesting from a number of perspectives. First, some scholars argue they are part of China's effort to advance its international agenda. In the case of Iran, China is seeking to establish a long-term relationship because of its future need for oil imports.[16] In the case of sales to Pakistan, it is argued, the agenda is to strengthen the primary enemy of China's longtime adversary, India.[17]

More directly interesting to this discussion, however, is the mechanism by which these sales were accomplished. Though there can be some debate, each of these sales arguably violates, or comes very close to violating, international agreements—the Nuclear Non-Proliferation Treaty (NPT) and the Missile Technology Control Regime (MTCR). As a result, the sales should have triggered a U.S. law that would impose trade sanctions against China. The Clinton administration chose not to impose such sanctions, however, in part because it accepted the Chinese government's contention that the sales were made by PLA-related companies, partially for their own profit, without the knowledge of the central government.[18] The U.S. government thus seems to accept China's contention that its central government cannot control the actions of some elements of the government even in matters as sensitive as the sale of nuclear weapons technology to pariah states.

If the claims of the Chinese government in this case are to be accepted, some elements of the government in China seem to be clearly above Chinese law. This being the case, is it realistic to expect the central government to be able to control the actions of central government actors, let alone provincial governments, in commercial agreements? The experience of the intellectual property agreement would indicate the answer is no.

## Piracy on the Seas

Piracy of intellectual property is not the only kind of piracy on the rise in the greater China region. More traditional piracy, the boarding of ships and theft of their cargo, is also on the rise. In some cases, the ships are taken and their crews killed. The ships are then repainted, renamed, and resold. More commonly, the seagoing equivalent of a mugging takes place; the ship is boarded, crew and passengers are robbed, and easily carried off cargo is stolen.[19] In one particularly troubling set of incidents of this type in 1996, a number of reports emerged of piracy by PLA boats in waters off southern China.[20] Exact statistics on this new wave of piracy are unavailable, but naval authorities from countries in the region, such as the Philippines and Taiwan, insist it is on the rise.

This topic may also seem, at best, tangentially related to the topic at hand. There is, however, a connection. Many of the stolen ships have been taken to Chinese ports for repainting and refitting. Chinese authorities have refused to cooperate in efforts to return the stolen property and prosecute the pirates. More troubling, many of the pirate boats, including one that engaged in a gun battle with the Filipino navy, bear the marks and carry the flags of Chinese navy vessels. Many victims of piracy report that the pirates are wearing Chinese military uniforms.[21]

Of course, piracy is illegal under both international and Chinese law. The failure of Chinese officials to cooperate in combating piracy, let alone the apparent involvement of the Chinese military in the piracy, is a chilling example of the problems that can emerge in a society without the rule of law.

## The McDonald's Lease

When it opened its operation in China, the McDonald's corporation, a U.S. fast-food purveyor with a worldwide presence, built a 700-seat establishment in Beijing only a short walk from Tiananmen Square on the ineptly named Avenue of Eternal Peace. McDonald's, a company with wide experience operating overseas, seemed to have done everything right. It had worked closely with Beijing city and central government officials and had obtained an "unbreakable" twenty-year lease before it opened in 1992.[22]

Imagine McDonald's surprise when only two years later the political winds shifted and it was told its Beijing lease would be terminated in order to make room for a new $1.2 billion office project. The reasons given for breaking the lease were unspecified "serious economic offenses." The company soon felt pressure to comply with the order, pressure applied by the cutoff of water and electricity and other problems with city officials.[23]

The real reason for the change in sentiment toward McDonald's was apparently a Hong Kong millionaire, Li Ka-Shing. Li had a wide range of holdings in China, including a Chinese electronics company. His business partners included a number of the well-known princelings. Li apparently decided that his latest venture, an office building complex to be known as Oriental Plaza, was best erected on the cite now occupied by McDonald's. In order to clear the way for the venture, he enlisted the support of many of his business partners and Beijing city officials. His campaign apparently proved more persuasive to Beijing city officials than McDonald's unbreakable lease.

Fortunately for McDonald's, the story does not end here. McDonald's enlisted the support of the U.S. government and foreign investors to fight Li. Eventually, the high-profile counterattack resulted in Li Peng, China's premier, heading a commission to investigate the matter; several Beijing city officials, including a deputy mayor, were arrested in an anticorruption campaign. In the end, the McDonald's lease held.[24]

Other western businesses, however, have not always been so fortunate. Despite McDonald's ultimate victory, the incident demonstrates that leases and other legal agreements provide only limited protection at best if the political winds begin blowing the wrong way. As one analyst commented at the time: "In China, there is no one crowd that can guarantee your success."[25]

### Establishing a Rule of Law

These four very different examples demonstrate a few of the ways that China's lack of a rule of law complicate its establishment of economic relations with others. Any manager from a western business operating in China could also add many other examples. Establishing a rule of law is not primarily a business or economic relations problem. It is a problem that affects all dimensions of international relationships with China and, on an even more fundamental level, the relationship between Chinese citizens and their government. In fact, it can be said that although the lack of rule of law is a complication for business and economic relations, often a serious complication, it is a matter of life and death for Chinese citizens.

Although they did not use the term, many of the concerns raised by the protesters at Tiananmen Square could be called rule-of-law problems. Qiao Shi's views on this rule-of-law problem were quoted at the beginning of this section. But his views are shared by a number of Chinese dissidents. For example, leading dissident Wang Xizhe wrote: "Over the past ten or so years, what Chinese people say in private about their government has become increasingly bold, their criticism of China's rulers increasingly sharp. They are becoming more disdainful of the leadership's authority and more doubtful of its legitimacy ... most of it is a reaction by the Chinese people to the Communist Party's dictatorial rule over the past several decades."[26]

## Rule of Law and Commerce

The efforts at political reform in China could help ease its integration into the world economy. In the meantime, however, the lack of a rule of law in China poses very concrete problems for business and economic ties with China.

During the debate on the North American Free Trade Agreement (NAFTA), Senator Daniel Patrick Moynihan (D-NY) was fond of posing the question in connection with Mexico: "How can you have free trade with a country that is not free?" Moynihan's argument, as explained more fully in other speaking and writing, was that Mexico was ruled by single political party, the PRI; lacked the democratic tradition of the United States; and had a judiciary completely controlled by the PRI.[27]

There is some evidence of real political reform in Mexico, but the argument made in connection with NAFTA is a valid one. Imagine a U.S. business that had somehow come into the disfavor of the PRI attempting to establish itself in Mexico. Its efforts could be blocked by PRI-appointed bureaucrats, and the PRI-appointed courts would merely uphold the decisions. The company could try to enlist the aid of the U.S. government and take the matter to a NAFTA dispute settlement body, but there are problems with this approach. Typically, the problems of a single company are not of a magnitude such that countries would expend their diplomatic resources and trigger international dispute settlement procedures to protect them. Further, international dispute settlement bodies are not set up to replace national courts; they are not equipped to review all the decisions of regulatory bodies in regard to a particular company. Traditionally, they focus only upon the acceptability of broad national laws.

If this argument has some merit with regard to Mexico, it has even more applicability to China. In China there is not even the facade of multiparty democracy. As noted, the power of the government or, more precisely, the leaders of the government is nearly unchallenged by either courts or a legislature. Hypothetically, if a particular western company were somehow to offend Jiang Zemin to the point that he was willing to make a personal effort to eliminate its Chinese operation, no observer would give that hypothetical business much chance of prospering in China. As discussed in the previous chapter, the list of potential tactics an angry leader could use range from power and water cutoffs, to failure to protect intellectual property, to exposing the venture to direct piracy. As the example of the McDonald's lease demonstrates, unless other Chinese political forces come strongly to a beleaguered business's aid, it would certainly be doomed; such is the power of leaders in a society without rule of law.

### Corruption and Bribery

The McDonald's example also brings into focus another element of the problem inherent in the lack of rule of law: bribery and corruption. Again, as most businesses operating in China will volunteer, bribery in China can take many forms. It ranges from small bribes to customs agents to expedite import clearance to similar bribes to local officials to ensure police attention.[28] Efforts to involve princelings in ventures in order to ensure favorable government attitudes toward new ventures can be viewed as a more subtle version of the same behavior; in a society without rule of law it is necessary to buy friends to survive.

Of course, the problem of corruption is not unique to China. It is found at some level in all countries and normal commerce can function in spite of it. In a country without rule of law, however, bribery can proceed on a much larger scale.[29] As the four examples at the beginning of this chapter illustrate, some form of corruption is usually at the heart of commercial problems caused by the lack of rule of law in China.

In recent Chinese history there have been countless anticorruption campaigns. These usually amount to one faction accusing another, usually correctly since the practice is widespread, of some form of corruption. The unintended result of these crackdowns, however, is to illustrate just how widespread the problem of corruption is in China.[30]

## *International Agreements and Rule of Law*

For the sake of this discussion, the most important problem caused by the lack of rule of law in China relates to China's apparent inability to keep the international commitments it makes in trade negotiations. China's dismal record in enforcing the international commitments made on intellectual property, as well as Chinese law on the subject, was discussed in the introduction of this chapter. As U.S. trade negotiators have conceded, this problem is probably not yet behind the United States and China.

### *The 1992 Market Access Memorandum of Understanding [MOU]*

Unfortunately, the problem of noncompliance with international trade agreements is not limited to intellectual property. In 1992, the Bush administration attempted to negotiate a market access agreement with China as well as an intellectual property agreement. After a drama involving threats of retaliation similar to those that played out on intellectual property, the Chinese agreed to open their market in four important ways. First, China committed to make its trade regime more transparent. Before they could be enforced, all trade laws and regulations were to be made publicly available. This was aimed at the problem of Chinese ministries declaring trade regulations as being for "internal use only" and, thus, not available to the companies affected by them. It was also aimed at preventing new, unannounced trade barriers from proliferating. Second, China agreed to sharply cut back on the number of products the government required licenses to import. Third, quotas, tariffs, and other import controls were to be pared back. Finally, arbitrary and unscientific standards for imported products and onerous certification requirements were to be eliminated or reformed.[31]

Some of the problems addressed by the Bush agreement were mentioned in the last chapter; others will be fully discussed in the next. For the purposes of this chapter, however, the main goal is to assess the degree to which China complied with the agreement. In its official assessments of the agreement from 1992 onward, the Office of the USTR has given China credit for substantial compliance with the agreement, while noting problems. For example, the latest National Trade Estimate (NTE) notes: "China has also taken steps to implement its commitment in the 1992 bilateral market access MOU to eliminate specified import restrictions no later than the end of 1997."[32] Unfortunately, as the "specified import restrictions" have been eliminated, others have often been raised. Four examples illustrate the problems of implementation with the 1992 agreement, referred to in government documents as the 1992 Memorandum of Understanding (MOU).

First, China did take steps to phase out some import licensing requirements. Simultaneously, however, MOFTEC has made two large categories of imports subject to "automatic registration requirements," which are functionally identical to import licenses. As the NTE notes:

> Despite steps China has taken under the bilateral MOU to eliminate licensing requirements, in early 1994 China issued two catalogues— one for electrical and machinery products, and another for general commodities—listing products that are now subject to "automatic registration requirements" and quota administration. The implementation of this registration requirement appears to pose a new de facto licensing requirement for products covered in the catalogue.

Several hundred products which had license or quota requirements removed pursuant to the MOU are now subject to the registration requirement.[33]

Second, as noted in the previous chapter, China committed in the 1992 MOU to end the practice of import substitution—substituting domestically produced products for imports. Recent industrial plans, however, have included new import substitution requirements. The NTE states:

> upon signature of this market access MOU in 1992, China confirmed that it had eliminated all import substitution regulations and policies and that it would not subject any products to import substitution measures in the future. . . . Despite this commitment, in 1994 China announced an automotive industrial policy that included clear import substitution requirements. This policy, designed to foster development of a modern automobile industry in China, explicitly calls for production of domestic automobiles and automobile parts as substitutes for imports, and establishes local content requirements which would force the use of domestic products, whether comparable or not in quality or price.[34]

Third, one of the simplest, but potentially most significant provisions of the 1992 MOU has not been fully implemented—the requirement that all regulations and laws impacting trade be made public. The Clinton administration has given the Chinese government credit for publishing many laws and regulations, but there are important exceptions. For example, at this writing, the electronic industry plan mentioned in the last chapter has never been published; information on the plan is taken from Chinese press accounts. Nonetheless, China appears now to be implementing the plan. Another important violation of the transparency commitment concerns government procurement. To again cite the NTE:

> China's government purchasing actions and decisions are subject to China's general laws, regulations and directives. Despite its commitment under the 1992 market access MOU to publish all laws and

regulations affecting imports and exports, some regulations and a large number of directives have traditionally been unpublished ("for internal use"), and there is no published, publicly available national procurement code in China.[35]

A fourth notable apparent violation of the 1992 MOU concerns the transfer of technology. In order to secure access to technology, China has frequently imposed a performance requirement upon foreign businesses operating in China that technology be transferred. The 1992 MOU includes a bar on the conditioning of import licenses upon the transfer of technology, which the continuing performance requirements violate, at least in principle.[36]

The 1992 MOU is an extensive agreement that covers many hundreds of different provisions of Chinese law and regulations. As the NTE points out, some portions of the agreement have been faithfully implemented by the Chinese. At minimum, the record of implementation for the 1992 market access MOU is much better than the record of implementation of the two intellectual property understandings, but that is more a comment upon the near total failure of the intellectual property agreements than a positive comment on the market access MOU. In general, there have been two problems with the 1992 MOU. First, as is discussed in the next section, China maintains so many overlapping and duplicative barriers that eliminating one or two layers does not truly open the market.

The second problem with the 1992 MOU, one more relevant to this chapter, is that the government of China has sometimes simply phased out one generation of trade barrier to erect a new similar one. The new "automatic registration requirement" or de facto import license is the clearest example. In the next chapter, which discusses formal trade barriers in more depth, there are several examples of similar replacement of one barrier with another. This effort to erect new barriers, coupled with new import substitution requirements and failure to make the Chinese trading regime transparent—all direct violations of the 1992 MOU—raises serious questions about both the willingness and the ability of the Chinese government to implement the 1992 MOU.

## Textile Transshipment

In addition to the intellectual property agreements and the 1992 market access MOU, the United States and China maintain one other major bilateral trade agreement—the textile import limitations negotiated under the Multi-Fiber Arrangement (MFA). The MFA is a special arrangement established parallel to the General Agreement on Tariffs and Trade (GATT) to control trade in textiles.

Textiles have an interesting history in connection with the GATT. While a full history of textiles and international trade is well beyond the scope of this book, suffice it to say that the major trading countries decided decades ago that textiles were so politically sensitive and so involved in developed–developing country or North–South trade that they could not be treated like other classes of goods. As a result, the MFA was established. Simply put, rather than allowing the market to work, the MFA establishes a rubric under which major textile-importing countries, such as the United States and countries within Europe, negotiate import limitations with textile-exporting countries.[37]

As a result of the MFA, textile trade is controlled by a complex series of country-specific and product-specific quotas. As part of the Uruguay Round negotiations, which created the WTO, the entire MFA system is being phased out over a period of ten years.[38]

To this background on the MFA, one complication must be added. Though not a member of the GATT and not yet a member of the WTO, China is the world's largest textile exporter and it has been a member of the MFA since 1984. Thus, the United States and China have negotiated a series of complex bilateral quotas under the auspices of the MFA.[39]

Clearly, the MFA bilateral understandings are somewhat different than the intellectual property agreements and the 1992 market access MOU. While the intellectual property agreements and the 1992 MOU are aimed at opening China's markets to U.S. exports, the MFA agreements open the U.S. market to China (or limit Chinese exports to the United States).

Despite this distinction, however, the MFA accords are binding international agreements. Whatever the problems with the MFA system (some have argued it harms U.S. consumers),[40] the MFA agreements are still negotiated in good faith and the United States has good reason to expect China to abide by them. Even if the MFA system is a bad one, the agreements with China are part of a global framework and, if China violates its commitments, the interests of other textile-exporting countries are harmed, in addition to those of U.S. textile producers.

Unfortunately, it appears that China has violated its MFA commitments to the United States and perhaps to other countries on a massive scale. In order to circumvent the import limits agreed upon under the MFA, China has apparently resorted to mislabeling and illegal transshipment of textiles. When the Chinese allocation for some classes of apparel are exhausted, Chinese producers illegally label their textile production as having originated in other countries, usually Hong Kong or Macau (a small Portuguese colony bordering China with a history and likely future that closely parallels Hong Kong). These mislabeled textiles are then illegally exported to the United States or other countries for which China has already met its import limits.

The U.S. Customs Service has taken action several times against China for textile transshipment. A number of raids have been conducted, fines and other penalties levied, a list of the companies involved in the violations has been published, and deductions have been made from China's MFA limits. Most observers from both China and the United States agree that illegal transshipment is a problem that involves a large volume of Chinese textile exports. One U.S. Customs Service investigator estimated that the level of illegal transshipment could approach $10 billion.[41]

The Chinese government responds to these charges by noting that they are the result of private companies attempting to circumvent the MFA, not the Chinese government. There is some truth to this claim, but most of the companies involved have ties to the government. Further, the Chinese government does have the responsibility to fulfill its commitments, and there is no evidence of any real effort by the Chinese government to control transshipment. Given the enormous control the Chinese government has over the Chinese economy and the activities of Chinese citizens, Chinese government claims of inability to control this problem simply ring hollow. (A new agreement was negotiated to control Chinese textile exports to the United States in early 1997. It remains to be seen whether China will make a serious effort to enforce this agreement.)

Unfortunately, the problem is not even limited to MFA transshipment, intellectual property agreements, and the 1992 market access MOU. China has reportedly also been less than diligent in enforcing commitments made to stop export of goods made with prison labor,[42] and on the pricing of satellite launch services.[43] At least in recent years, China's has failed to keep its commitments in international trade agreements more often than it has kept them. Enforcement problems have grown so serious and so widespread as to call into question the wisdom of expending the effort to negotiate further agreements with China.

The problem deserves special attention in the context of China's integration into the world economy. It is legitimate to ask why the United States and other countries should invest the time and effort in negotiating complex and difficult trade and economic arrangements with the Chinese when China has such a poor record of keeping the international arrangements it reaches. A sounder approach might be to call a halt to further negotiations until China fulfills its current commitments.

Certainly, without either some dramatic action on the part of its trading partners or dramatic change within China, there is no reason to believe that China will be more diligent in enforcing future multilateral agreements than it has been in enforcing existing bilateral ones. Potentially of more concern, the United States and other countries may have fewer options for responding to

China's violations of multilateral agreements than is the case when current bilateral agreements are violated. This topic is discussed in more detail in Part III. From the perspective of the topic of this chapter, the lack of respect for the rule of law internationally and the apparent bad faith shown in recent negotiations is another serious problem created by China's lack of rule of law.

## Conclusion

Upon reading the preceding analysis, many observers will accurately respond that China is not the only country lacking a reliable rule of law. Bribery, corruption, and the concentration of power in leaders and not in the law are problems that can be found in many countries, including many that play at least minor roles in multilateral economic institutions. The problems with China are distinct for two reasons, however. First, given the size of the Chinese economy, it is impossible to ignore problems that might raise less concern with minor players. Frankly, if a country has only a small economy, many otherwise significant problems can be ignored with little practical impact. The same cannot be said with regard to China.

Second, the degree of the problem in China is without parallel. With regard to enforcement of trade commitments, it can be said that China ignores its trade commitments more often than it keeps them. Coupled with experiences in other areas, such as sale of nuclear materials, legitimate questions can be raised as to whether the Chinese government is even capable of keeping any of the agreements it makes. This is an especially serious concern in cases in which elements of the government have some financial incentive to violate the agreement. Until China performs better in honoring its commitments, it can be argued that it is better to keep a country with such little regard for the rule of law outside the global trading system rather than bring it in and undermine the credibility of the system. This issue is also discussed in more detail in Part III.

At minimum, however, it seems entirely reasonable for the world to insist upon two conditions related to rule of law before proceeding with further international agreements aimed at integrating China into the world economy. First and foremost, China must demonstrate a record of keeping the international agreements it makes. If it takes China some time to establish such a record, efforts aimed at integration should be slowed down. After all, China should not be brought into the global trading system and other world institutions until it is willing and able to shoulder the responsibilities that accompany such an important role.

Second, China must establish a minimally reliable method for enforcing its own laws. For the reasons detailed earlier, without such a system China simply cannot be a stable and reliable member of the world economic community. On a positive note, there are signs of progress on this front. In addition to the statements of Qiao and other prominent Chinese, the Chinese courts have recently upheld several suits aimed at enforcing Chinese intellectual property laws. It is too early to make anything approaching a final determination of the importance of these court decisions, but they are encouraging

It is important to keep in mind that the primary beneficiaries of the establishment of rule of law in China would be the Chinese people. As advocates of change, like Qiao Shi, have argued, such a step is necessary to establish a stable and equitable society. Establishment of rule of law with regard to commerce will also be essential to ensuring a continued flow of foreign investment, which has become critical to the Chinese economy. In recent years, the excitement about the future prospects for the Chinese economy convinced many western companies to invest in China. In the last two years, the rate of growth of foreign investment has slowed markedly; western business seems to be looking for other investment options and expressing concern over Chinese investments. High-profile instances of ignoring the rule of law with regard to commercial ventures, like the McDonald's incident or failure to protect intellectual property, could further sour foreign investors and harm the Chinese economy.

For its own sake then, as well as for the sake of other countries and the world economy, the Chinese government would be well advised to listen to its internal calls for the establishment of rule of law. In this case, political reform and entry into the world economy are not only compatible but mutually beneficial.

## Notes

1. Yasheng Huang, "Why China Will Not Collapse," *Foreign Policy,* June 22, 1995, 54.

2. Willy Wo-Lap Lam, "Qiao's Bid for the Throne," *South China Morning Post,* April 3, 1996, 21.

3. Tony Walker, "Chinese Rivals Use Western Press to Air Differences," *Financial Times,* September 11, 1996.

4. United States International Trade Commission, *Foreign Protection of Intellectual Rights and the Effect on U.S. Industry and Trade: Report to the United States Trade Representative—Investigation 332–245,* (Washington, DC: United States International Trade Commission, 1988).

5. Greg Mastel, *American Trade Laws after the Uruguay Round* (Armonk, NY: M.E. Sharpe 1996), 46–48.

6. See, for examples, Peter Behr, "For U.S. Firms in China, Obstacles and Opportunity," *Washington Post,* September 1, 1994.

7. For a full description of legal changes, see *Memorandum of Understanding Between the Government of the People's Republic of China and the Government of the United States of America on the Protection of Intellectual Property,* 1992.

8. International Intellectual Property Alliance, *1995 Special 301 Recommendations and Estimated Trade Losses Due to Piracy,* Submission to the United States Trade Representative, February 13, 1995, 1–10.

9. "Clinton Hails Copyright Accord with China," *Asian Economic News,* June 24, 1996.

10. *Inside U.S. Trade,* an Inside Washington Publication, July 12, 1996, 31.

11. David E. Moore, "Keep It Cool," *International Business,* June 1996.

12. Stefan Halper, "China on a Roll . . . over Us?" *Washington Times,* May 29, 1996.

13. Bill Gertz, "Iran Gets China's Help on Nuclear Arms; US Report Indicates Technicians Will Visit Tehran to Work on Uranium Plant," *Washington Times,* April 17, 1996.

14. "China and MFN," *Financial Times,* May 21, 1996.

15. Jim Hoagland, "On China: The Surest Way to Fail," *Washington Post,* May 19, 1996.

16. Kent Calder, "Asia's Empty Tank," *Foreign Affairs* (March/April 1996), 55–69.

17. R. Jeffrey Smith, "Washington's 'Bermuda Triangle of News,' " *Washington Post,* May 31, 1996.

18. Steven Erlanger, "U.S. Won't Punish China Over Sale of Nuclear Gear," *New York Times,* May 11, 1996.

19. Graham Hutchings, "China's Sea Mafia Rules Asia's Waves," *Sunday Telegraph,* April 7, 1996, 24.

20. "Manila Still to Rule Out Chinese Role in Clash," *Reuters World Service,* January 29, 1996.

21. Ibid.

22. Mark Tran, "Big Mac Incident Marks Decline in U.S.-China Trade," *The Guardian,* December 5, 1994, 12.

23. Glenn Gale, "McCracking the Whip over GATT," *South China Morning Post,* December 5, 1994.

24. Lee Han Shih, "Li Ka-shing Suffers Major Setback in China Corporate Scene," *Business Times,* February 27, 1995, 22.

25. Michael Steinberger, "Sweet Turns into Sour for Li Ka-shing," *The Times,* May 26, 1995.

26. Wang Xizhe, "The Voices Beijing Is Desperate to Still," *Washington Post,* November 17, 1996.

27. Senator Daniel Patrick Moynihan, Debate on Extension of Fast Track Procedures, *Congressional Record,* May 23, 1991, S6597.

28. Nancy Zucker Boswell, *Book 'Em Danno! Combating Government Bribery and Corruption Overseas* (Washington, DC: Economic Strategy Institute, 1996).

29. The WTO is now considering negotiations aimed at global curbs on bribery. Hopefully, this will lead to the problem being addressed in a larger context.

30. BBC, "China's Anti-Corruption Campaign Featured," *BBC,* October 7, 1996; Xinhua News Agency, "Enforcement Proposals on Anti-Corruption Drive Raised," *Xinhua News Agency,* March 9, 1996; Uli Schmetzer, "China's Campaign to Rout Corruption Brings Down Ex-Beijing Mayor," *Chicago Tribune,* September 29, 1995; Seth Faison, "China's Selective Anti-Corruption battle; A Few Top Officials Are Laid Low, but Graft Is 'Everywhere,' " *International Herald Tribune,* August 11, 1995; and "The Politics of Corruption," *Economist,* May 20, 1995.

31. *Memorandum of Understanding Between the Government of the United States of America and the Government of the People's Republic of China Concerning Market Access,* 1992.

32. United States Trade Representative, *1996 National Trade Estimate Report on Foreign Trade Barriers* (Washington, DC: USTR, 1996), 48.

33. Ibid., 46.

34. Ibid., 50.

35. Ibid., 51.

36. *Memorandum of Understanding Between the Government of the United States of America and the Government of the People's Republic of China,* Article II, 1 (iv), 1992.

37. For background on the MFA and its impact see Giogio Barba Navaretti, Riccardo Faini, and Aubrey Silberston, *Beyond the Multifibre Arrangement* (Paris, France: OECD Publication, 1995).

38. *Final Texts of the GATT Uruguay Round Agreements,* "Agreement on Textiles and Clothing."

39. Brenda A. Jacobs, "Textiles and Apparel Trade under the WTO," *China Business Review* (March/April 1995), 35–38.

40. William R. Cline, *The Future of World Trade in Textiles and Apparel* (Washington, DC: Institute for International Economics, 1990).

41. "China: U.S. Customs Says Illegal Textile Transshipments Are Larger than Original $2 Billion Estimates." *SAM Trade* (May/June 1995), 13.

42. Daniel Southerland, "U.S., China Sign Prison Labor Pact," *Washington Post,* August 8, 1992.

43. United States Trade Representative, *1996 National Trade Estimate Report on Foreign Trade Barriers* (Washington, DC: USTR, 1996), 40.

# 6

---

# Trade Barriers

Formal trade barriers, like tariffs, quotas, and import licenses, are the most visible impediment to free economic interchange with China. In practical terms, it is almost impossible to disentangle the problems caused by trade barriers from those related to the sweeping powers of the totalitarian government or the limitations on foreign currency exchange. The limitations on trading rights, for example, which were discussed in the context of the totalitarian government system in China, are also formal trade barriers. Similarly, the administered import demand procedures are implemented through formal trade barriers.

Chinese trade barriers not only duplicate the effects of other policies, they also duplicate other trade barriers. The entire Chinese trade regime is characterized by multiple layers of duplicative trade barriers. It is not unusual for imports of a particular product to be blocked by a prohibitive tariff, an administrative import quota, import licenses, and a restrictive certification regime. Individually, any one of these barriers would be sufficient to exclude imports from China. Often the differing levels of protection are the result of different Chinese ministries seeking authority over import decisions.

The overlapping barriers do, however, make trade, trade negotiations, and the task of trade liberalization quite complex. As was noted previously, the problem is similar to that with Japan; the layering of trade barrier upon trade barrier makes the task of opening the market much like the task of peeling an onion—peeling away one layer merely reveals another. Thus, a trade agreement that merely removes one barrier has almost no practical effect upon trade.

The 1992 market access MOU attempted to resolve this problem by addressing a wide range of barriers simultaneously. In addition, the MOU required that all barriers be made transparent to ensure that the onion did not secretly grow new layers as some were peeled away. Unfortunately, this effort was not entirely successful; the onion has proven very adept at growing new layers. Although hundreds of trade barriers have been eliminated as a result of both MOU and China's own efforts at trade liberalization, the ultimate effect on trade is unclear for two reasons. First, many of the barriers that were eliminated had little practical effect on import access to the Chinese market because other barriers acted to exclude imports once the initial barrier was eliminated.

Second, while China has been eliminating some trade barriers it has been raising others. China's new system of automatic registration requirements to replace import licenses is one of the most obvious examples in this regard, but there are others. For example, China recently imposed a new series of restrictions on foreign news services operating there; the most onerous of these forces news services to clear their stories through their state-run competitor, the Xinhua News Agency.[1] Though China has hinted at flexibility on this issue, China has not withdrawn the proposed policy change. Restrictions have also emerged to deny U.S. films promised access to the Chinese market.[2] Though real progress has been made in liberalizing a few sectors to trade, the combined effect of the new trade barriers and new industrial plans frustrates true liberalization of the Chinese trading regime. In recent years, it has not been clear whether the net effect of all of these changes has been a more open Chinese market or not.

As noted, rumors have recently circulated that China is contemplating major reforms in its foreign trade regime. Chinese officials, however, denied these rumors. Only time will tell if there is substance to these reports.

## Tariffs

In China as in all countries, the most obvious trade barriers are tariffs—direct taxes upon imported products. Tariffs are easily understood and their effects well known. Tariffs are also an important part of China's import regime, though perhaps not the most important.

At 35 percent, China's average tariff is high from the perspective of most major trading countries.[3] Major trading countries, like the United States, countries within Europe, and Japan, maintain average tariffs in the low single digits. Chinese officials point out, however, that this is a poor comparison to draw given China's level of development. It is difficult to decide what group of trading countries would be best thought of as China's peers, given its unique success in industrialization and exporting while serious development problems remain. Nonetheless, it is fair to say that many industrializing countries that are WTO members do retain average tariff rates into the 20 percent range and higher.[4]

With considerable fanfare, China announced its intention at a meeting of the Asia-Pacific Economic Coordination (APEC) group to cut 4,000 tariffs. These cuts would bring China's average tariff rate to 23 percent in 1996 and 15 percent in 1997. It later turned out that rather than being new cuts these were the same tariff cuts previously promised in the context of WTO accession negotiations. After the announcement, China was notably slow in releasing the details of the planned tariff cuts. There were stories of great internal debate over the makeup of the list of tariffs to be cut. As the situation stands, MOFTEC is to release the announced tariff cuts in several tranches.[5] Some of the announced cuts have materialized. Hopefully, further promised cuts will be forthcoming.

In addition to maintaining a high average tariff, the Chinese tariff schedule also contains many "spikes," or prohibitively high individual tariffs; certain tariffs have been, until recently, as high as 150 percent. For example, the tariffs on fruit juice are as high as 55 percent depending upon the type of juice. There is a 75

Table 6.1

**Selected Chinese Tariffs** (tariff spikes)

| Item | MFN rate (%) | General rate (%) |
|---|---|---|
| Nightshirts and pajamas (man-made material) | 40 | 130 |
| Porcelain ceramic articles | 55 | 100 |
| Computer keyboards and Mouses | 20 | 40 |
| Universal signal generators | 50 | 80 |
| Four-wheel-drive cars | 120 | 270 |
| Bicycles | 50 | 130 |
| Pencils and crayons | 50 | 80 |
| Pocket lighters | 60 | 130 |
| Pipes | 60 | 130 |
| File cabinets | 30 | 80 |
| Glass beads | 40 | 100 |
| Yarn | 30 | 70 |
| Footwear uppers | 60 | 100 |
| Enameled cast-iron | 30 | 100 |

*Source: China's Tariff & Nontariff Handbook* (Manassas, VA: U.S.-China Information & Service Corporation, 1996).

percent tariff on beer and mineral water. Light fixtures face a 40 percent tariff and many auto parts, such as shock absorbers, face a 55 percent tariff.[6] A list of some other tariff spikes is found in Table 6.1. In some cases, such as auto parts, these high tariffs complement Chinese industrial policy. In others, however, such as mineral water, the motive for the markedly high tariff is unclear.

Chinese officials are quick to point out that the official tariff bears little resemblance to the actual level of tariff assessed. Their are two primary reasons for the discrepancy. First, customs officials are known to "negotiate" the actual tariff assessed.[7] The tariff charged in one Chinese port can be different from the tariff for the same product in another port. Official connections and bribes are said to play a role in these "negotiations." Second, China has had a long-standing policy of allowing foreign joint ventures to import production equipment duty free. Much to the chagrin of foreign investors, China recently announced that it has ended this program. Thus far, protests against this decision have fallen on deaf ears. Chinese officials argue that such special incentives for foreign investment are no longer needed and that the Chinese government needs the tariff revenue.[8]

Nonetheless, as a result of these tariff breaks the actual level of tariff assessed is often somewhat lower than the official rate. The actual level of tariff charged is impossible to determine given the ad hoc nature of the "negotiations" to lower tariffs. A Chinese official recently cited a story in the Chinese official press suggesting that the actual level of tariff assessed on imported products might be as low as 5 percent.[9] Yet this seems to be more of an off-the-cuff guess than an actual estimate, and no supporting methodology has been supplied. Further, reports from those actually trying to import into China suggest a considerably higher tariff.

Closely linked to the issue of tariffs are special value-added taxes, luxury taxes, and other fees collected primarily on imported products. The NTE notes on this topic:

> In addition to import tariffs, imports may also be subject to value-added and other taxes. Such taxes are to be charged on both imported goods and domestic products, but application has not been uniform, and these taxes may be subject to negotiation. China has used the combination of tariffs and other taxes to clamp down on imports that officials viewed as threatening domestic industries.[10]

**Import Quotas, Licenses, and Other Restrictions**

In addition to tariffs, Chinese imports are limited by an array of nontariff barriers, including quotas, import licenses, and registration requirements. As discussed in Chapter 2, section 1, most of these import limitations function to limit imports to "demanded" levels as determined by government agencies, most notably the State Economic and Trade Commission, the State Planning Commission, and MOFTEC.[11] These nontariff barriers are simply the tools used by the Chinese government to exercise control over commerce; in other words, the tools of economic planning. Trading rights, which can be used to completely bar imports or exports of a particular product or to keep a particular entity out of foreign commerce, serve a similar function as another check to ensure the government can control international commerce.

It may seem odd that the Chinese government should choose to employ a trading regime with so many duplicative measures to control imports. The layer upon layer of barriers seems to go far beyond what would be required to practice simple protectionism. Indeed, this perception is correct. Even Chinese government entities complain about the difficulty of obtaining needed imports on occasion.[12] Part of the answer for the overlap is bureaucracy. Individual ministries often have control of particular policy tools and not others. Thus, although the diverse trade barriers have the same effect—blocking imports—individual barriers are controlled by different ministries. A universal characteristic of bureaucracies is that they are unwilling to cede power easily. Therefore, the duplicative import barriers remain in place because bureaucracies are striving to preserve turf.

Import licenses are a good example. MOFTEC controls the issuance of import licenses. MOFTEC officials assert that once other agencies in the Chinese government have authorized the import of particular products, import licenses are automatically issued. Still, import licenses are required for imports of fifty-three categories of products ranging from consumer goods to raw materials. All told, about 50 percent of imported products require import licenses.[13] As mentioned in the previous chapter, MOFTEC agreed to phase out import licenses only to issue a new requirement of automatic import registration for large classes of products, which had the same effect.[14] Apparently, the bureaucrats at MOFTEC were not ready to cede influence over import decisions.

Frequently, the ministries involved directly in the production of particular types of products have a role in determining whether imports of competing products will be allowed.[15] Without casting aspersions on any industry within the United States, it is reasonable to assume that if domestic industries could determine if and when competing imports would be permitted, there would be fewer imports into the United States as well. The same is likely true for most countries, and it is true in China. In China, however, industries are actually partially given this power through their parent ministries; protectionism is the demonstrated result.

## Standards, Testing, and Certification

Other common tools of protectionism are standards, testing, and certification requirements. In the guise of pursuing laudable objectives, such as consumer and environmental protection, governments bent on protectionism often impose unreasonable and scientifically baseless requirements on imported products. Though not the primary tool of protectionism in China, standards, testing, and certification problems do arise. For example, imported manufactured goods are required to obtain a quality license before they can be sold to Chinese consumers.[16] Depending upon the product and the Chinese ministries involved, these quality licenses can be quite difficult to obtain.

Most of the import problems in this category arise because of a classic "fox guarding the chicken coop" problem. Given the nature of the Chinese economy, the ministries with expertise in particular industries understandably set standards for imports in that sector. As a result, the Ministry of the Chemical Industry (MCI) sets standards for imported chemicals, the Ministry of the Electrical Industry (MEI) sets standards for electronic products, and so on. This is all sensible enough, but, as noted in the previous section, in China these ministries are often in the business of producing those very products. Allowing them to set standards on imports gives them a golden opportunity to restrict the competition.

Standards, testing, and certification requirements have been a particular problem in the chemical sector. In 1994, for example, the MCI issued a draft regulation for imported chemicals requiring that a sample of any proposed imported chemical, its formula, a statement of proposed uses, and a list of potential

customers be provided to MCI before the chemical could be imported.[17] Obviously, the material MCI required in order to certify
imports also amounted to a full business plan for producing the
chemical; since MCI is in the chemical business, this caused
understandable concern. The more onerous features of this particular regulation were beaten back, but U.S. chemical companies
report that meeting all of China's import tests generally requires
about $5 million per agricultural chemical.

Imported automobiles have also faced expensive certification
requirements.[18] Although the regulations are apparently undergoing
some revisions, companies seeking to export autos to China must
provide two automobiles for testing and pay for Chinese inspec-
tors to visit manufacturing facilities. This is all to meet Chinese
safety and environmental standards, which are considerably looser
than those of the United States or other western countries. Western countries frequently recognize the work of foreign safety and
environmental tests rather than requiring independent tests.

Standard and certification issues have been a particular sore
point between the United States and China in the agricultural
area. A long list of products has been subject to such restrictions.[19]
For example, China has blocked imports of wheat from western
U.S. ports because of concern over a wheat fungus that the U.S.
Department of Agriculture believes has long been controlled.

## Government Procurement

In most trading countries, government procurements or government purchases of goods and services provide an enticing market
for imported products. China provides unique challenges and opportunities with regard to government procurement. Since the
government in China is involved in more activities than it is in
most countries, and since China is growing at a breakneck pace
and building major infrastructure, government procurement opportunities are enormous. In fact, a number of foreign companies
have done well in securing contracts for major government procurement projects, such as subway construction.[20]

Unfortunately, governmental barriers do restrict foreign companies seeking a share of China's government procurement market. Although China has promised to make government procurement procedures and all other trade regulations publicly available, it has not fulfilled this commitment.[21] Ministry regulations on government procurement are often kept confidential. To add to the complexity of the process, provincial governments as well as central government entities are often involved in major procurement decisions. The ministries involved are often very protective of their prerogatives regarding government procurement and maintain tight control of the process of putting contracts up for bid.[22]

Given problems in other areas, it is not terribly surprising that bribery and corruption also seem to play a role in government procurement decisions. Reportedly, the princelings are frequently involved in government procurement decisions. Privately, some Chinese officials also complain about the regulation of government procurements. They explain that it is more a problem of corruption than an effort at protectionism. Companies with friends on the "inside" win procurement contracts while other Chinese companies, the Chinese government, and ultimately Chinese citizens pay a heavy price.

This explanation has a ring of truth and is consistent with what is known about Chinese business practices in other areas; problems in the government procurement sector may have more to do with the lack of a rule of law than with protectionism. Nonetheless, since foreign companies have fewer friends on the "inside," they are particularly hard hit by government procurement corruption.

## Subsidies

Since China is still a partially nonmarket economy, it is not surprising that government subsidies to business ventures constitute another class of trade barriers. China claims that most of its direct export subsidies have been phased out.[23] In late 1995, China even suspended, and perhaps eliminated, the practice of rebating taxes paid on products that are exported.[24] Many analysts felt that this decision would lead to a sharp decrease in Chinese exports. Some measures of China's trade performance, such as the trade balance with the United States, did show a disruption for several months, but Chinese exports seem to be recovering.

Subsidies, however, go far beyond the Chinese government's narrow definition of export subsidy. The Chinese government still directly owns many enterprises. Depending on the definition used, the state-owned enterprise (SOE) sector is still responsible for one-third to one-half of China's GDP.[25] SOEs enjoy many benefits from the state, including loans at interest rates far below market rates and other financial subsidies, both direct and indirect. In fact, after years of trying to wean SOEs from dependence on the government, China is budgeting additional aid to them. Not surprisingly, given the large number of Chinese citizens employed by SOEs, their future remains a topic of intense debate in China. The debate is mostly conducted behind closed doors and out of the public eye, but sometimes shows up in publications like the latest five-year plan and in occasional comments in the Chinese press.[26]

Subsidies are not limited to SOEs. Almost all enterprises operating in China enjoy some benefits that are classified as subsidies under U.S. trade law and international agreements. The prices of energy, raw materials, and labor, in most sectors, are set by the government at considerably less than world market rates.[27] Given the relative isolation of the Chinese economy and the many remnants of the communist system, many other subsidies likely remain. Chinese officials are fond of making the claim that 90 percent of the products in the Chinese economy have prices at least partly determined by the market.[28] If this claim is to be accepted, it can also be assumed that 10 percent of prices are set entirely by the government, not the market. Further, since the price of so many basic inputs are set by the government, it is fair to assume that only a very small percentage of goods, if any, have their prices set entirely by the market.

Subsidy-related problems are at the heart of another U.S.-

Table 6.2

**Comparison of Top Respondent Countries of Dumping Complaints (Cases Filed), 1984–1993 and 1994–1995**

| Country | 1984–93 | 1994–95 |
|---|---|---|
| Japan | 62 | 7 |
| Korea | 40 | 3 |
| Taiwan | 40 | 2 |
| Brazil | 37 | 7 |
| Germany | 29 | 2 |

*Sources:* U.S. International Trade Commission, *Annual Report 1993, 1994;* USITC, *Operation of the Trade Agreements Program,* 1985–93.

China, and increasingly EU-China, trade dispute. China has become the leading target of antidumping complaints in the United States. U.S. anti-dumping laws have a long and controversial history, but are based on principles set out in the GATT and later in the WTO (see Table 6.2). In essence, antidumping laws, which are maintained by the United States and most other trading countries, provide for imposition of offsetting duties on imported products that are sold either at less than their price in the home market or at less than their cost of production. In recent years, the number of successful U.S antidumping cases involving Chinese products has skyrocketed.[29] China is now far more frequently the target of U.S. antidumping actions than Japan, Korea, or any of the traditional targets of the law. Further, the dumping margins placed upon Chinese products are often very high, frequently in excess of 100 percent.

This explosion of antidumping complaints involving China is a side-effect of Chinese subsidies. With energy, raw materials, and labor all subsidized by the government, the cost of production of goods in China often bears little resemblance to their actual market cost of production. In addition, as the World Bank has noted, China has often directed state trading companies, which export most Chinese-made goods, to export regardless of price to fill hard currency quotas.[30] The combined effect is that when antidumping actions are filed against Chinese-made imports, dumping margins are almost always found.

China has complained loudly about the number of antidumping actions brought against Chinese goods in the Untied States and Europe.[31] The antidumping complaints, however, are just another manifestation of the problems of integrating a large non-market economy—which does not fully rely upon the price mechanism—into the market trading system.

Chinese subsidies also pose a serious barrier to integrating China into the WTO. One of the areas in which the WTO improves upon the GATT is in the discipline of subsidies. Although the GATT prohibited export subsidies, the practical discipline of most domestic subsidies (also known as production subsidies) was left primarily to offsetting duties imposed by the importing country on subsidized products. The WTO, however, greatly tightened limits on subsidies.[32] Although precise figures are difficult to obtain on the level of subsidies provided to Chinese SOEs,[33] they almost certainly exceed WTO permissible subsidy levels. The government provision of other inputs is also likely to run afoul of the WTO, unless China undertakes major reforms.

### Service Barriers

Up to now, most of this discussion has focused on trade barriers aimed at blocking imports of goods. Imports of services, however, such as insurance or financial services, actually face more barriers.

This is not atypical. For a variety of historical reasons, in most countries, service markets are more restricted than goods markets.[34] Goods have generally been more easily portable than services and thus more frequently traded. It is one thing to export an automobile or a toaster oven to a foreign market, but quite another to export legal or financial services. In addition to confronting the unique professional standards for service providers, often established to protect local service providers, there is the problem that many services simply do not travel well. Architects, lawyers, and doctors generally do not work long distance. The service provider often needs to be either on site or near site. Because of the natural difficulties in trading services, the GATT trading rules were never extended to services. In the negotiations to establish the WTO, the first steps were taken to apply some of the basic free-trading principles to trade in services.[35]

China is no exception to the global pattern of restricted service markets. Foreign service providers have extremely limited access to the Chinese service markets. Often, outside access is restricted through special license arrangements that allow only a single foreign service provider in a service market, such as insurance or accounting services.[36] The foreign service providers that are allowed to do business in China are often restricted to a single region or even a single city. Central and provincial governments also impose a variety of other difficult restrictions upon foreign service providers to ensure Chinese service providers are not driven from the market by stronger foreign competitors.

In spite of all of these restrictions, foreign service providers have made some headway in China. Though subject to significant restrictions, as of early 1996, 137 foreign banks were operating in China.[37] Many of these banks simply followed other foreign companies with which they had a business relationship to China, but some are attempting to provide services to Chinese customers. In the insurance field, some foreign companies have made notable headway. One American company—AIG—has established an impressive foothold in southern China.[38]

## Protection of Intellectual Property

The long and troubled history of U.S.-China negotiations aimed at the protection of intellectual property was discussed at length in the previous chapter. It is worth noting, however, that the lack of effective protection in China is a problem that goes well beyond the entertainment and computer software industries. Many manufacturing companies have had their trademarks infringed in China. Piracy of patented chemicals, drugs, and trade secrets has become a widespread problem.[39] Several companies that rely heavily upon intellectual property have declined to establish ventures in China because of the threat of piracy.

In interviews for the preparation of this book, U.S. companies confided that, despite grandiose initial objectives of tapping the booming Chinese market, the primary purpose of their present ventures in China is to keep bootleg copies of their products from being exported to other Asian markets. The Chinese market itself is essentially written off to piracy.

In sum, intellectual property piracy is so widespread that it is a barrier to western businesses establishing operations in China. The threat of piracy is particularly serious to smaller companies that lack the resources, contacts, and political influence in and out of China to combat piracy of their trademarks, trade secrets, and products. Beyond that, no foreign business is so powerful that the threat of intellectual property piracy does not figure into corporate decision making regarding China.

## Investment

One of the primary reasons that China has erected and maintained such a wide array of trade barriers is to encourage foreign companies interested in operating in China to pursue an investment strategy rather than an export strategy. In other words, the high trade barriers encourage companies interested in selling their wares in China to produce them there through joint ventures or other investments as opposed to merely exporting to China from distant markets. This is a strategy that many countries have pursued over the years; it is premised on the notion that, if foreign companies are going to sell in the market, they should be forced to provide employment for the local populace. It also dovetails nicely with the conventional business wisdom that market conditions often force local investments to support a continuing business relationship.

Given the torrent of foreign investment China has absorbed in recent years, the strategy can be declared a success. The combination of the attractive Chinese market or, at least, the future market and China's trade barriers has given outsiders powerful incentives to invest in China. Most major western companies, involved in everything from the production of cellular phones to fertilizer, have felt the need to invest in China.

Through a variety of formal and informal practices, China has strongly encouraged and even insisted that most of those investments take the form of joint ventures involving a Chinese partner. Foreign companies, often seeking partners with local expertise, have been willing to enter into such arrangements. As a result, the joint venture has become the preferred method of entering the Chinese market in most sectors.

To encourage foreign investment, China has amended its laws to provide more protection for foreign investments against obvious threats, such as nationalization.[40] In the current environment, however, these threats seem of little immediate concern.

Of greater concern is a new set of foreign investment guidelines issued by the Chinese government in June 1995.[41] The guidelines make it clear that investment is no longer as welcome as it had been only a few years ago. They divide the economy into three general categories. First are sectors in which investment was permitted and usually encouraged. These tend to be industrial sectors in which China had not established a presence and looked to western investment as a source of know-how and technology. Second are sectors where investment was permitted, but often restricted. These tend to be sectors in which China is concerned that foreign competition might destroy domestic Chinese industries or in which China is pursuing an industrial policy. Third are sectors where investment was prohibited. This category tends to include sectors in which there is extreme concern for protecting domestic Chinese ventures, such as some service sectors, or sectors in which China believes foreign investment may threaten national security or state control; this includes telecommunications and broadcast ventures.[42]

Chinese investment policy is changing as China's industrial strength improves. As the country has gained a stronger foothold in many sectors, however, it has become less accepting of foreign joint ventures or, at least, has come to require more of the foreign partner. In sectors in which investment was previously encouraged, China has become more demanding. In the automobile sector, for example, the joint ventures that were welcomed with open arms only a decade ago are now being criticized for merely building cars from kits without sufficient Chinese content. This is in spite of the fact that foreign joint ventures maintain Chinese content of 60, 70, and even 80 percent and have invested significant technology and training in Chinese operations.[43] In its automotive industrial policy and in other government pronouncements, China has made it clear that investments in the automotive sector must bring sophisticated production technology, such as drive train construction, to China in order to be welcome.[44]

In interviews conducted in preparation for this book, Chinese officials indicated that they look to venture with foreign automotive companies to bring new technology to China and that they will count their automotive plan a success only if Chinese-owned automotive companies are able to command a strong share of the market. These statements will doubtlessly cause concern for automotive companies with investments in China. Unfortunately, there is good reason to believe that China will also raise the requirements on foreign investments in other sectors as it gains strength and confidence in them. It is clear that China's government planners see foreign investment as a tool to help achieve China's industrial policy goals; this is bad news for foreign ventures looking for a long-term role in China.

As part of the effort to ensure that foreign ventures "bring something to China," performance requirements are often inserted into the contracts establishing joint ventures with foreign entities. Performance requirements stipulate that the foreign partners in joint ventures must fulfill certain obligations in order to launch and operate the joint venture. Some of the more common ones include requirements that production technology be transferred, that a fixed and usually very high percentage of production be exported, and that the ventures import less than they export to ensure a positive contribution to China's foreign exchange and trade balances.

Again, as noted in a previous section, these performance requirements seem to violate both bilateral agreements and the investment protections included in the WTO. The EU has become particularly concerned with addressing the export and foreign exchange balancing requirements in WTO negotiations. U.S. negotiators have raised the issue of technology transfer requirements.[45]

Clearly, these performance requirements distort trade patterns in both the long and the short term. In fact, that is their primary purpose. Other countries have pursued similar strategies in the past, and the major trading countries have largely ignored the efforts because they were often viewed as too insignificant to bother with, although performance requirements did provide the impetus for the investment protections in the WTO. China, however, presents a unique case. The enormous leverage the Chinese market provides and the Chinese government's willingness to use performance requirements on a sweeping scale create the potential that trade patterns and comparative advantage will be severely distorted by these requirements to the detriment of China's trading partners. No other single issue deserves more attention in trade negotiations than performance requirements in terms of both their immediate effects and the potential for future problems.

## Conclusion

There has been considerable debate recently as to whether the current level of protectionism in China is higher or lower than that of other countries widely regarded as protectionists. Comparisons are most frequently made with Japan and Korea.[46] Some defenders of China's trade practices have gone so far as to suggest that China's economy is, in fact, more open than that of Japan and Korea at comparable times in its development;[47] this is a surprising claim and it is usually advanced without meaningful supporting evidence. The argument that China is an open market has three important flaws.

First, there is no accepted single measure of openness or even an accepted definition of the term. Trade balances are not a good measure. Under appropriate economic conditions, it is entirely possible for a die-hard protectionist to run a trade deficit or for a free trader to run a trade surplus.[48]

Imports as a percentage of GDP or total trade have more potential but also face serious limitations. For example, economies dependent upon the import of raw materials, such as Japan, will appear to be more open to imports than they truly are if the raw material imports dictated by natural resource endowment and not trade policy are included in the calculation. Also, large, diversified economies, such as the United States, will tend to import less than smaller, more specialized economies. This is not the result of protectionism but a predictable consequence of a diverse economy. In other words, diversified economies make a larger percentage of the products they consume than more specialized economies.

The second weakness in the reasoning of those who claim China's economy is more open than Japan's and Korea's is that they may mistake differences in economic strategy for true openness. Japan has a long history of excluding foreign interests, including foreign businesses. Japanese firms have historically joined together in business groups, known as *keiretsu,* and refused to do business with foreign companies.[49] Korea has followed a similar pattern. Using this closed home market as a base, Japan and Korea have focused on developing selected industries into export powerhouses.[50] The Japanese automotive industry and the Korean steel industry are two of the success stories produced by this strategy.

China emerged as a player in the world economy decades later, however, and had more ground to make up given the time lost in the long experiment with Maoist socialism. China found, as Japan did at one point, that foreign firms could provide a jump start for Chinese industry through technology and know-how gained in joint ventures.

Many take China's openness to and, in fact, aggressive pursuit of foreign investment as a sign that it is following a liberal trade strategy. Historically, economies that have allowed liberal access to foreign investors have often established a liberal trading regime. This historic connection is likely due to two factors. First, economies willing to allow liberal foreign investment generally had a liberal economic philosophy that included openness to imports. Second, foreign investors often became a significant political force that advocated openness to imports within these countries.

There is no reason, however, to assume that this pattern will be repeated in China. As this chapter should make clear, the current Chinese regime does not have a liberal attitude toward trade and seems to be becoming more skeptical of foreign investment. Second, given the nature of the political system, it seems very unlikely that foreign investments will be able to gain much direct political influence in China. Thus, China may be an entirely different case; its apparent openness to foreign economic ties as demonstrated by a willingness to allow foreign investment does not necessarily indicate an economic philosophy that is fundamentally more open to trade than those of Japan and Korea. It is entirely possible that when China began to enter the world economy, it was forced to pursue a different economic strategy, which emphasized foreign investment. As it develops, however, this philosophy could prove every bit as exclusionary as those of Japan and Korea. The tightening of restrictions on investment and the recently unveiled Chinese industrial plans seem to indicate movement in this direction.

Third and finally, as was noted in the opening section, there are disturbing and apparently conscious parallels between China's current economic strategy and those of Japan and Korea. As noted in Chapter 1, section 1, given China's double-digit growth rate, conventional economic theory would hold that China should be importing far more and running a large trade deficit. China's deficit has, however, always been very small, and for the past two years China has run a sizable trade surplus that is projected to continue. When these economic conditions are factored in, China's current economic and trade performance is, in fact, disturbingly similar to that of Japan in a similar period.

In the end, however, little can be gained by continued focus upon the comparison between China, Japan, and Korea. The three countries are different. They have different business cultures and different economic strengths and weaknesses. Further, they face different economic constraints and challenges. All that can authoritatively be said is that they are relatively closed markets. The United States, the world economy, and the citizens of those three countries would be better off if each adopted a more open trading regime.

Unfortunately, Japan and Korea were integrated into the world trading system at a time when little attention was given to ensuring that countries practiced free trade. Other geopolitical objectives were given higher priority. The world economy has suffered as a result. Hopefully, the world has learned from the mistakes made with Japan and Korea. The trading community has a unique historic opportunity to convince China to adopt a more liberal trading regime as the price of entering the trading system. There is no reason that past mistakes need be repeated; this opportunity should be grasped regardless of them.

## Notes

1. United States Trade Representative (hereafter USTR), *1996 National Trade Estimate Report on Foreign Trade Barriers* (Washington, DC: USTR, 1996), 56.

2. International Intellectual Property Association, *1995 Special 301 Recommendations and Estimated Trade Losses Due to Piracy,* Submission to U.S. Trade Representative, February 13, 1995, 2–3.

3. USTR, *1996 National Trade Estimate,* 49.

4. Ibid.; average tariff levels are listed for all major countries.

5. Ibid.

6. Specific tariff levels taken from U.S.-China Information and Service Corporation, *China's Tariff and Non-Tariff Handbook* (Manassas, VA: Self-published, 1996).

7. USTR, *1996 National Trade Estimates,* 49–50.

8. Ibid., 50.

9. Ibid., 49.

10. Ibid., 46–47.

11. Ibid., 47.

12. Ibid.

13. Ibid., 47–48, and U.S.-China Information and Service Corporation.

14. USTR, *1996 National Trade Estimates,* 48.

15. Ibid., 47.

16. Ibid., 50–51.

17. Adhoc Chemicals Group, *Letter to Song Jiam State Councilor Protesting New Chemical Import Regulations,* August 5, 1994.

18. USTR, *1993 National Trade Estimate Report on Foreign Trade Barriers* (Washington, DC: USTR, 1993), 54.

19. USTR, *1996 National Trade Estimate.*

20. For a brief discussion see Rahul Jacob, "Asian Infrastructure: The Biggest Bet on Earth," *Fortune,* October 31, 1994, 139–50; "Asian-Pacific Brief: Guangzhou Subway Project," *Asian Wall Street Journal,* December 22, 1993.

21. USTR, *1996 National Trade Estimate,* 51–53.

22. Ibid.

23. Ibid., 53.

24. Ibid.

25. For discussion, see World Bank *Bureaucrats in Business: The Economics and Politics of Government Ownership,* a World Bank Policy Research Project (Oxford: Oxford Press for World Bank, 1995).

26. Matt Forney, "Trial by Fire," *Far East Economic Review,* September 12, 1996, cover story.

27. USTR, *1996 National Trade Estimate,* 53.

28. Reference to this claim is noted by Nicholas Lardy, *China in the World Economy* (Washington, DC: Institute for International Economics, 1994).

29. Greg Mastel, *American Trade Laws after the Uruguay Round* (Armonk, NY: M.E. Sharpe, 1996), 81.

30. World Bank, *China: Foreign Trade Reform,* a World Bank Country Study (Washington, DC: The World Bank, 1994), 110–26.

31. Nigel Holloway, "Sweet Smell of Excess: China Says It Is Unfairly Targeted by U.S. Dumping Law," *Far Eastern Economic Review,* September 5, 1996, 16–18.

32. *Final Texts of the GATT Uruguay Round Agreements,* Agreement on Subsidies and Countervailing Members, April 15, 1994.

33. Joyce Barnathan and Dexter Roberts, "A Hard 'Soft Landing,' " *Business Week,* October 21, 1996, 51–52.

34. USTR, *1996 National Trade Estimate,* 55–56.

35. Ibid.

36. Ibid.

37. Ibid.

38. "China Capital Beijing to Open Service Sector More: Report," *Dow Jones Business News,* September 26, 1996.

39. International Intellectual Property Alliance, *1995 Special 301 Recommendations.*

40. USTR, *1996 National Trade Estimate,* 57.

41. Ibid.

42. Ibid.

43. Greg Mastel, "Sober Look at China Investment," *Journal of Commerce,* October 18, 1996.

44. USTR, *1996 National Trade Estimate,* 50.

45. Ibid., 50, 57.

46. Lardy, *China in the World Economy,* 35–38.

47. Ibid.

48. Greg Mastel and Andrew Szamosszegi, "America's New Trade Nemesis," *International Economy* (May/June 1996), 24–27.

49. For discussion, see Chalmers Johnson, *Japan: Who Governs?* (New York: W.W. Norton, 1995).

50. Ibid.; and Kihwan Kim and Danny M. Leipziger, *The Lessons of East Asia. Korea: A Case of Government-Led Development,* a World Bank Publication (Washington, DC: The World Bank, 1993).

# 7

## Foreign Exchange Restrictions

The problems that trade barriers or totalitarian government policies pose for China's integration into the world economy are relatively simple for the layman to understand. The problems posed by China's controls on foreign exchange and international financial transactions are a bit more difficult for noneconomists to grasp, however. Many even find the topic intimidating. Certainly, the economics of exchange rates and international finance are intimidating topics, but the problems caused by Chinese policies in this area are among the key hurdles that must be confronted in order to integrate China into the world economy, and they are integrally related to other problems.

In fact, as a recent U.S. Department of the Treasury report on this topic put it:

> Treasury believes that foreign exchange restrictions form an integral part of China's overall trade regime. As such, these restrictions cannot be separated from larger trade questions affecting U.S.-China economic relations. Easing restrictions on access to foreign exchange would represent a step toward liberalizing China's trade regime, reducing the bilateral trade imbalance, and improving economic relations between China and the United States.[1]

For western businesses operating in China and western governments, there are two particularly important implications of Chinese foreign exchange controls. First, government controls on foreign exchange are a practical barrier for foreign companies seeking to repatriate profits from China or otherwise move funds in and out of China. Second, from the perspective of the world economy, China's managed exchange rate provides Chinese authorities with a potentially powerful tool for manipulating foreign exchange to create a favorable trade balance. Even relatively small exchange rate movements can have the effect of making exports less expensive, in effect creating a subsidy, and making imports more expensive, imposing an effective tariff. This is why the U.S. government has directed the U.S. Treasury Department to issue a biannual report on the efforts of foreign governments, including China, thought to be manipulating currency values in order to create a trade advantage.[2]

On a positive note, while Chinese policy has made little progress and, in some cases, actually moved backward in other areas, real progress has been made with regard to foreign exchange. Only a few years ago, China actively used foreign exchange policy to achieve goals like improving trade balances and blocking repatriation of profits. Although the potential still exists for more of this foreign exchange mischief, Chinese foreign exchange policy does seem to be moving in the right direction. China has even committed to the goal of full convertibility of the Chinese currency, the yuan or RMB. This would place Chinese foreign exchange policy on a par with that of other economies. Still, until convertibility is achieved, Chinese policies in this area will raise serious questions, and there is always the potential for slippage.[3]

### Restraints in the Chinese Foreign Exchange System

The Chinese foreign exchange system is tightly controlled by the government. Over the years, China has employed four primary policy tools that must be considered in any analysis of the system. Some of these tools have recently been limited by Chinese directives, but, in order to understand the operation of the system, it is first necessary to discuss these basic mechanisms.

First, the exchange rate for China's currency, the yuan or RMB, to foreign currencies is still held near a predetermined level controlled by the government. Since currency swap markets have been established, the government's ability to set exchange rates independent of the marketplace has been reduced and the influence of the market in setting exchange rates has increased. Through mechanisms such as convertibility controls, foreign exchange restrictions, and government intervention, however, the government still maintains substantial control of the exchange rate for the yuan.

In contrast, most major currencies, like the U.S. dollar, the German mark, and the Japanese yen, float freely on currency markets rather than being pegged. The free-floating exchange rate allows currency adjustments to take place daily or hourly to reflect underlying economic changes. In theory, floating exchange rates should allow currency adjustments to eliminate large current account deficits or surpluses.

In very simple terms, the mechanism works as follows. If country A is running a trade deficit, it will create an excess of country A's currency in world markets because the currency is being spent to purchase goods from other countries. The surplus of country A's currency in world markets will make it of less value compared to other currencies (currency markets work on the same basic mechanism as goods markets, so an oversupply will tend to push down prices) and it will depreciate. This depreciation will make country A's exports less expensive and its imports relatively more expensive. In time, this should eliminate country A's trade deficit.[4]

Of course, this example is oversimplified. Other factors can create demand for country A's currency, such as international financial transactions using country A's currency or borrowing from abroad by country A. Currency markets have also been known to fluctuate dramatically in response to market concerns raised by international events.[5]

Because of these and other complications, the major governments of the world instruct their central banks to intervene in currency markets in order to manage exchange rates. Therefore, it is more accurate to describe the current system for setting international exchange rates as a managed floating system rather than a free-floating system.[6] Nonetheless, the central point remains; exchange rates for major currencies are allowed to adjust on an almost instantaneous basis to reflect changes in competitiveness, trade balances, and a myriad of other factors.

Before adopting the current floating exchange rate system, the major economies of the world, acting through the International Monetary Fund (IMF), attempted a fixed exchange rate system. Different rates of inflation sometimes changed real exchange rates (a topic that will be covered in some detail later), but the nominal exchange rate was fixed, unless adjusted by an official rate change. That system broke down for reasons beyond the scope of this discussion, but experience with fixed exchange rates demonstrated that there was great potential for countries to fix the exchange rate for their currency at an artificially low level to create a permanent trade surplus.[7]

Fixed exchange rates can thus be a powerful tool of mercantilism, which is why China's system of very tightly managed exchange rates attracts particular concerns since China is running a trade surplus at a time when a large deficit would be expected. Recently, China has held the yuan/U.S. dollar exchange rate at something over 8 yuan to the dollar. China has allowed its relatively high inflation to reduce the real exchange rate. This occurs because China's annual inflation rate has run ahead of that of the United States; thus, at the end of the year the 8.3 yuan will buy less relative to the dollar than it would at the beginning of the year. Since the exchange rate is held near 8 yuan to the dollar, however, 8 yuan will still exchange for one U.S. dollar. As a result, the yuan does appreciate in real terms.[8]

Many relatively small economies peg their exchange rates to major currencies because they are concerned about currency market fluctuations buffeting their economies and because their currencies are simply not widely enough used to be traded on a world currency market. Therefore, pegging, in and of itself, is not prima facie evidence of currency manipulation. A number of countries, however, including South Korea, Taiwan, and China, have been accused by the U.S. Treasury Department of manipulating foreign exchange to achieve trade gains.[9] In China's case, there seems to be no practical reason why China could not adopt a much more liberal foreign exchange system. The only barrier seems to be the attitude of the Chinese government.

A second policy tool sometimes used by the Chinese government is differential or dual exchange rates. Dual exchange rates operate by exchanging yuan for foreign currency at one exchange rate for certain activities and at another rate for other activities. It is an obvious tool for effectively subsidizing some activities, such as investing in desired sectors, while effectively discouraging others.[10] Dual exchange rates are a clear distortion of the market.

A third frequently used tool has been limitation of the times, places, and amounts of foreign exchange that foreign firms can obtain. Again, this is a clear market distortion. This mechanism, in conjunction with other policy tools in this section, allows China to control the movement of capital in and out of China, including repatriation of profits. Of course, it does not provide total control. As the World Bank has noted, capital does flow between China and Hong Kong through unofficial channels. Still, foreign exchange controls provide an alternate tool for managing the exchange rate of the yuan. The government has also used its tight control of the foreign exchange system as a tool to control behavior of foreign firms operating in China.[11] For example, foreign firms can be denied foreign exchange until or unless performance requirements are fulfilled.

Finally, perhaps the bluntest tools in this arsenal are foreign exchange balancing requirements. As discussed earlier, these are normally inserted into contracts with foreign joint ventures to ensure that the joint ventures result in a net inflow of foreign exchange to China either by exporting more than they import or through new foreign investment funds. Clearly, foreign exchange balancing requirements distort the function of the market.[12]

## Timeline of Reform

For some time, foreign governments and foreign investors have criticized these Chinese foreign exchange policies. China has responded with promises of reform, and the reform has come, albeit slowly and at an uncertain pace.

In one important initial step, after years of complaints, China ended the dual exchange rate in January of 1994.[13] In this move, China retired one of its most onerous foreign exchange tools after years of service.

In April of 1994, China launched a more sweeping set of foreign exchange rate reforms. The heart of these reforms was the establishment of a foreign currency market in China through a mechanism known as an interbank swap market. The Foreign Exchange Trading Center (FETC) is centered in Shanghai, but banks around the country participate. The swap market allows yuan to be exchanged for foreign currencies and increases liquidity for foreign commerce.[14]

In July of 1996, China announced that foreign firms would be allowed to participate directly in the swap market. Previously, foreign ventures' access to the swap market was tightly restricted. Foreign firms were only allowed access to the swap market after gaining approval from the State Administration of Exchange Control (SAEC). The SAEC often conditioned access to the swap market and thus repatriation of profits on the foreign ventures having fulfilled requirements, such as meeting foreign exchange balancing requirements. Reportedly, the leverage of access to the swap market was also used to extract new concessions from foreign firms.[15]

In connection with the announcement of foreign participation in the swap market, the Chinese government also announced plans for further foreign exchange reforms. Nineteen ninety-seven was set as the target date for allowing full convertibility of yuan for current account transactions, chiefly trade transactions.[16] Given the array of other trade and foreign exchange controls still in place, full convertibility for current account purposes is a fairly modest step. China can still retain control of the flow of goods and the related flow of capital through policy tools discussed in previous chapters, so the exposure should be limited

At the same time, China announced that it did not plan to allow full convertibility of the yuan for capital account purposes, such as international borrowing and investment, for at least another ten years.[17]

In the meantime, other controls would continue to operate, and the People's Bank of China, China's central bank, would continue to manage exchange of the yuan. Outside observers, such as the U.S. Treasury Department, refer to the operation of the People's Bank in controlling the yuan as a managed float. The term, however, probably suggests a much more liberal arrangement than actually exists. Working from the basic peg to the U.S. dollar, the market exchange rate is allowed to move a maximum of plus or minus .25 percent. Each day the People's Bank posts a new exchange rate that is the average of the previous day's transactions.[18]

It is worth noting that the People's Bank of China also maintains a complex and nontransparent system for setting interest rates, which has the potential to contribute to foreign exchange problems. China has maintained relatively high interest rates for most purposes to dampen inflation. Of course, this also affects foreign trade by, among other things, limiting demand for imports and changing demand for the yuan. In the SOE sector, however, China has set a lower interest rate to avoid further SOE layoffs. Some observers believe that it will not be possible to maintain a differential interest rate in the SOEs over the long term.[19]

## Continuing Concern?

As noted above, despite China's continued use of a controlled exchange rate, inflation rates have resulted in a real appreciation of the yuan. Further, many of the interventions of the People's Bank are aimed at strengthening the yuan, not weakening it.[20] Over time, this should prevent China's current account surplus from growing too large. Still the government-managed system does inhibit the market from bringing about full adjustment in the Chinese trade and current account balance. As is discussed below, the fixed exchange rate is also a factor that has kept the Chinese trade deficit small and sometimes contributed to a Chinese trade surplus.

Another reason for concern is that the devil is often in the details in interpreting changes in Chinese policy. For example, it is difficult to assess the importance of China's recent announcement that foreign participation will be allowed in currency swap markets until all regulations are published and the system has operated for a time. For many years, the Chinese government has used access to foreign exchange as a key policy lever to control the operation of foreign firms. A number of tools, such as foreign exchange balancing provisions, are still in use. Against this background, there is reason to be somewhat skeptical of China's announced changes.

China's continuing reluctance to allow full convertibility of the yuan and to fully eliminate foreign exchange controls is cause for concern. As the quote in the introduction from the Treasury Department noted, current foreign exchange controls are largely duplicative of various trade barriers. Further, China currently enjoys a sizable trade surplus as well as a strong inflow of foreign investment. Finally, China has now amassed an enormous foreign exchange reserve in excess of $80 billion—one of the largest in the world (see Table 7.1 and Figure 7.1). Some critics have noted that not all of these reserves are held directly by the central bank.[21] This point is certainly correct, but by using the numerous policy tools at its disposal, the Chinese government still has access to the vast majority. This reserve should be more than sufficient to address foreign exchange or trade problems. Even against this backdrop, however, China still refuses to fully liberalize its foreign exchange system and retains government control of policy tools capable of distorting foreign exchange markets. This reluctance to fully liberalize even under excellent economic conditions raises real concern over the possibility of a resurgence of market-distorting foreign exchange controls if economic diffi-

Table 7.1

**China's International Reserves, 1980–1995** ($million)

|      | Total, less gold | Foreign exchange |
|------|------------------|------------------|
| 1981 | 5,058            | 4,783            |
| 1982 | 11,349           | 11,365           |
| 1983 | 14,987           | 13,476           |
| 1984 | 17,366           | 16,705           |
| 1985 | 12,728           | 11,913           |
| 1986 | 11,453           | 10,514           |
| 1987 | 16,305           | 15,236           |
| 1988 | 18,541           | 17,548           |
| 1989 | 17,960           | 17,022           |
| 1990 | 29,586           | 28,594           |
| 1991 | 43,674           | 42,664           |
| 1992 | 20,620           | 19,443           |
| 1993 | 22,387           | 21,199           |
| 1994 | 52,914           | 51,620           |
| 1995 | 75,377           | 73,579           |

*Note:* Until 1992, foreign exchange statistics include holdings of the Bank of China and the People's Bank of China. Beginning in 1992, Bank of China holdings are excluded.

Figure 7.1. **China's International Reserves, 1980–1995** ($million)

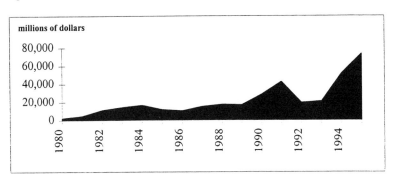

*Source:* International Monetary Fund.
*Note:* Until 1992, foreign exchange statistic include holdings of the Bank of China and  the People's Bank of China. Beginning in 1992, Bank of China holdings are excluded.

culties emerge. China still has the potential to manipulate foreign exchange markets to achieve trade advantages.

### Is China Manipulating Its Exchange Rate?
### A Sensitive Question

Out of concern that neomercantilist countries may manipulate the exchange rate of their currencies to gain trade advantages, the U.S. Congress instructed the Treasury Department in the 1988 Trade Act to monitor foreign countries thought to be engaging in this practice and report back to Congress. Initially, the attention of both the Congress and the Treasury Department focused on Korea and Taiwan, both of which engaged in questionable practices.

The Treasury Department, however, soon began to focus more attention on China. This quote from the July 1994 report to Congress is typical:

> Based on China's continued reliance on foreign exchange restriction that could limit imports, it is Treasury's judgment that China manipulates its exchange system to prevent effective balance of payments adjustment and gain unfair competitive advantage in international trade. Treasury urges Chinese authorities to eliminate the segmentation of the foreign exchange market and restrictions on access to foreign exchange. Such steps would facilitate imports and promote adjustment in China's large bilateral surplus with the United States.[22]

In the language of such reports, this was fairly pointed criticism of China. Chinese authorities reacted angrily; meetings were canceled and threats were made to the U.S. business community. Echoing the arguments made by Chinese authorities, a U.S. source even criticized the Treasury Department findings arguing that it was not credible to criticize China for manipulating its currency when it was running a global trade deficit.[23]

As discussed in earlier sections, this argument cannot survive careful analysis for two reasons. First, China has since amassed a sizable trade surplus, particularly with the United States. Second, it is just as possible for a country to manipulate its currency while running a trade deficit as it is to maintain trade barriers while running a trade deficit. Further, the trade advantages gained through running a smaller than expected trade deficit are just as real as those gained from an artificial trade surplus and just as damaging to the interests of trading partners and the world economy.

Despite this, the Treasury Department seems to have taken the criticism to heart. Only five months later, and after China's trade account began to move toward surplus, Treasury released the following toned-down statement:

> As noted in the July report, China has taken important steps to re-form its foreign exchange system this year, unifying exchange rates and liberalizing domestic firms' access to foreign exchange. Yet, government approval of foreign exchange purposes by foreign-funded enterprises, which account for a large share of China's imports, is still required. Documentation requirements for domestic enterprises wishing to acquire foreign exchange for current transactions are also burdensome and give authorities the scope to prohibit foreign exchange transactions. While approval is readily given at the moment, the arrangements can only be viewed as intended to provide the means to limit imports of goods and services if government authorities wish to do so. The non-transparency of the process and the criteria for approval allow scope for discrimination in imports. It is therefore Treasury's determination that China is not currently ma-nipulating its exchange system to prevent effective balance of pay-ments adjustment and gain unfair competitive advantage in international trade, but that it retains the capacity and bureaucratic means to do so in the future.[24]

The following year, China announced no further reforms and its trade balance moved strongly into surplus. Yet Treasury was still unwilling to again identify China as a currency manipulator under U.S. law as it had done previously. It did, however, include the following comment in its annual report:

> While we do not find that China is manipulating its currency as described in the statute, China's special circumstances merit addi-tional mention. In the absence of a well-developed capital market with market determined interest rates that provide a clear signal of domestic credit conditions, it is even more difficult than in most

countries to make a determination of the appropriate real exchange rate. Consequently, China's large and growing overall current account surplus and substantial bilateral surplus with the United States (discussed in detail in the August 1995 interim report) deserve careful monitoring.[25]

Aside from apparent sensitivity to criticism, it is difficult to understand what drove Treasury's decision to stop accusing China of manipulating its currency, but, as even Treasury concedes, the potential continues to exist for China to manipulate its currency. Until China undertakes fundamental reforms, that potential will exist.

## Conclusion

Despite the concerns expressed throughout this chapter, it is worth reiterating that China has taken positive steps to adopt a more open foreign exchange system. Regardless of the overall assessment of the Chinese foreign exchange regime, the abandonment of the dual exchange rate in 1994 and the increased access to foreign exchange granted to foreign firms are significant steps. Given current economic conditions, that movement could be more dramatic. Nonetheless, recent movements have been positive.

In other areas, it is difficult to give an optimistic assessment of the overall direction of Chinese policy, however, foreign exchange reforms have been encouraging. Unfortunately, on a cautionary note, these changes are reversible and there is real reason for concern that a shift in bureaucratic sentiments in response to changed economic or political conditions could wipe away much progress. As the Treasury Department has noted, the wisest course under present conditions is to continue to monitor developments and press for further reform.

## Notes

1. U.S. Department of the Treasury, *Report to the Congress on International Economic and Exchange Rate Policy* (Washington, DC: Department of the Treasury, May 1993), 25.

2. *Omnibus Trade and Competitiveness Act of 1988* (H.R. 3): Sec. 3004, International Negotiations on Exchange Rate and Economic Policies; and, Sec. 3005, Reporting Requirements.

3. U.S. Department of the Treasury, *Interim Report to the Congress on International Economic and Exchange Rate Policy,* August 1996, 11–13.

4. Robert Grosse and Duane Kujawa, *International Business Theory and Managerial Applications,* 2d ed. (Boston, MA: Irwin, 1992), 208.

5. Ibid., 223.

6. For discussion, see Kathryn M. Dominguez and Jeffrey A. Frankel, *Does Foreign Exchange Intervention Work?* (Washington, DC: The Institute for International Economics, September 1993).

7. Margaret Garritsen de Vries, "The Bretton-Woods Conference and the Birth of the International Monetary Fund," *The Bretton Woods–GATT System: Retrospect and Prospect after Fifty Years,* ed. Orin Kirshner (Armonk, NY: M.E. Sharpe, 1996), 3–18.

8. U.S. Department of the Treasury, *Interim Report to the Congress,* August 1996, 12; and U.S. Department of the Treasury, *Interim Report to the Congress on International Economic and Exchange Rate Policy,* August 1995, 22.

9. U.S. Department of the Treasury, *Interim Report to the Congress,* August 1996, 9.

10. Ibid., 31.

11. United States Trade Representative (hereafter USTR), *1996 National Trade Estimate Report on Foreign Trade Barriers* (Washington, DC: USTR, 1996), 59.

12. USTR, *1994 National Trade Estimate Report on Foreign Trade Barriers* (Washington, DC: USTR, 1994), 56.

13. U.S. Department of the Treasury, *Interim Report to the Congress on International Economic and Exchange Rate Policy,* July 1994, 25.

14. Ibid., 25–26.

15. Ibid., 25.

16. Wong Shiang-Way, "Call for Lower Forex Charges, More Stability" *South China Morning Post,* July 16, 1996.

17. Teh Hooi Ling, "China Not Ready For Full Convertibility," *Business Times,* July 5, 1996.

18. U.S. Department of the Treasury, *Interim Report to the Congress,* August 1995, 21.

19. USTR, *1996 National Trade Estimate Report,* p. 45.

20. Nicholas R. Lardy, *China in the World Economy* (Washington, DC: Institute for International Economics, 1994), 86–87; and Department of the Treasury, *Interim Report to the Congress,* August 1996, 12.

21. Lardy, *China in the World Economy,* 88–90.

22. U.S. Department of the Treasury, *Interim Report to the Congress on International Economic and Exchange Rate Policy,* December 1994, 29–31.

23. Lardy, *China in the World Economy,* 86–88.

24. U.S. Department of the Treasury, *Interim Report to the Congress on International Economic and Exchange Rate Policy,* December 1995, 13.

25. U.S. Department of the Treasury, *Interim Report to the Congress,* August 1995, 19.

# 8

## Additional Thoughts on Barriers to Integration

When asked to review some of the subject matter in Part II of this volume, a Chinese official expressed concern that the material chosen was too critical of China. Of course, this comment is predictable and even, perhaps, a job requirement. Nonetheless, the average reader might get the impression that the Chinese market is impenetrable and that the government of China is pursuing an unambiguously mercantilist policy that threatens the world economy.

This impression is not entirely fair. Chinese economic policy is different but not necessarily more threatening than that of many other countries. Its most disturbing aspect is a strong element of nationalistic mercantilism; unfortunate though it might be, this is shared by a number of countries. It is certainly an element of current Korean and Japanese policy. Though more liberal economic thinking is the rule in the western world, the comments of particular western politicians are probably not much different than those of Chinese government officials. Further, the underlying goal of Chinese officials is almost certainly advancing the lot of Chinese citizens to what they see as equal status with the rest of the world, as opposed to undermining western economies.

It is also worth noting that, although China is known for monolithic thinking, there is diversity of thought on economic issues in China. Some Chinese economic thinkers seem legitimately committed to economic reforms that could be helpful for China and the rest of the world. If successful, Qiao Shi's campaign for rule of law will improve the prospects for economic and trade relations with China while improving the rights and protections accorded to average Chinese citizens.

Further, despite the existence of many trade barriers, Chinese imports continue to grow. In the first half of 1996, Chinese imports grew more quickly than Chinese exports. Barring a major setback, China's total imports will soon top $150 billion.[1] In short, China does import.

Further, despite numerous restrictions and other problems, many western businesses have been successful in China. Many major western companies have established large and growing Chinese operations. Some western businesses with experience in both markets compare the business climate in China positively to that in Japan two decades ago when Japan was at a similar level of development.

All that said, current Chinese trade and economic policies pose real problems for its trading partners and complicate the task of integrating China into the world economy. Further, there are continuing indications of a real debate going on inside the Chinese government about the desirability of economic reform and growing dependence on western governments and foreign firms. If that debate were to shift, new protectionist and mercantilist policies could easily result. Already, ministries have succeeded in raising new trade barriers, barriers that often erase past progress even while China campaigns for membership in the WTO.

Of greater concern, China seems to have developed a neomercantilist economic policy built on exploiting foreign investors as a short-cut to production technology, a source of foreign exchange, a point of political leverage, and an access point for export markets. Clearly, Chinese policy makers have noted the successful policies of Japan and Korea and have borrowed liberally from those models. They have added to them an increased emphasis on foreign investment as a short-cut to developing strong domestic industries. The continued reliance upon economic planning indicates that the government plans to manage these industries, built with foreign capital and technology, into Chinese national champions that can eventually rival the world leaders.

The world economy was burdened and trade greatly distorted by the Japanese and Korean industrial policy efforts. In addition to imposing real costs on the rest of the world in lost industries and lost employment, and in distorting comparative advantage, the success of those policies has undermined the political consensus underpinning free trade and the global trading system. If the soon-to-be world's largest economy, China, follows the same course, it could simply be too much for the global market to bear. After World War II, the U.S. economy was powerful enough to purchase billions of dollars in Japanese imports allowing Japan to grow quickly, often at the expense of U.S. industries.[2] The United States does not have the economic strength or political desire to extend the same favor to China. No other country seems likely to voluntarily step forward to become China's developmental market. Today, to be politically and economically sustainable, an economic relationship must be reciprocal and built around free trade and economic interchange.

On a positive note, the United States and the world have the opportunity to build just that kind of economic relationship with China. There is no reason that past mistakes need be repeated. China's dependence on western markets and western capital gives the West great leverage to shape Chinese policy. Now, as China enters world economic institutions, is the time to use that leverage to ensure that past mistakes are not repeated.

### Notes

1. "China Says Imports to Reach $149 billion in '96," *Reuters*, September 7, 1996.
2. Clyde V. Prestowitz, *Trading Places* (New York: Basic Books, 1988).

# Part III

## Integrating China into the World Economy

As the preceding section should make clear, the task of integrating China into the world economy will not be an easy one. China maintains numerous policies that are simply not consistent with world standards. Solving some of these problems will require more than simply eliminating a few trade barriers; fundamental reform in China's legal system is required to create an economic system compatible with that of the rest of the world. Perhaps most difficult of all, China must transfer some of its reliance on the government to make decisions to reliance upon the market. Without a doubt, these reforms will be difficult for China, and the process of integration fraught with frustration and setbacks for all parties.

Nonetheless, it is a challenge that must be undertaken. Though the economic system remains underdeveloped in many respects and still too bound to a communist ideology, the Chinese economy has simply grown too large to ignore. China's growing economic strength coupled with its diplomatic influence and military power give both China and the world reason to work toward a harmonious integration. China needs access to global markets and continued outside investment to continue its meteoric economic growth. If this growth were to stall, unemployment and food shortages could flare into a serious political crisis. The rest of the world needs both access to China's promising future market and, more importantly in the short term, to ensure that Chinese economic policies do not cause disruptions damaging to global trade and other national economies.

Thus far, economic problems with China have been addressed on an ad hoc basis with occasional bilateral negotiations to address specific problems. As is discussed in more detail below, this approach can continue for a time without creating a crisis. Eventually, however, all of the world's major economies, including China, must be brought into the economic fold and assume the attendant responsibilities. In short, China cannot remain outside the system forever; eventually the problems will grow too large to be addressed in ad hoc negotiations.

The terms on which integration occurs, however, are critical. China must be brought into the world's economic institutions, like the WTO and perhaps eventually the G-7 and the OECD, in a manner that strengthens those institutions, not undermines them. In order to accomplish this task, China must undertake the economic, political, and legal reforms discussed in the previous section. Although it has expressed an interest in membership, China has thus far been reluctant to undertake further reforms. If China were to join without reform, it would essentially be allowed all of the benefits of membership without undertaking the most important responsibilities. Such an inequitable situation would burden the system instead of strengthening it.

At some point, China will likely seek membership in all major institutions, but it has thus far focused efforts on joining the WTO. China began its current membership campaign more than ten years ago when the WTO was still known as the General Agreement on Tariffs and Trade (GATT).[1] Recently, diplomatic developments have raised hopes that the terms for China's membership in the WTO could be set in 1997 or 1998.[2] Since it appears to be the most imminent step in the integration process, the following discussion focuses primarily upon the issue of WTO membership. The prospects and problems with WTO membership for China are analyzed, and a strategy for integrating China into the WTO and other institutions is outlined.

### Notes

1. For a timetable of related events see Nicholas R. Lardy, *China in the World Economy* (Washington, DC: Institute for International Economics, 1994), pp. 141–43.
2. Robert Kapp, "The Road To 'Normalization': U.S.-China Relations," *China Business Review*, July 1996.

# 9

# Why China Should
# Be Brought into
# the Trading System

Over the years, China's campaign for membership in the world
trading system has waxed and waned. When efforts initially began
a decade ago, they were pursued with considerable enthusiasm. A
working group was formed to consider China's application and a
number of meetings were held. It soon became clear, however,
that there were significant political and substantive reservations
on the part of a number of countries about China's membership
and that the process would be extended; China settled for observer
status in the GATT and membership in the Multi-Fiber Arrangement (MFA), which it had already achieved.[1] When the GATT was
being replaced by the WTO in 1994, China again mounted an
aggressive campaign to join the WTO as a founding member.
This effort, however, failed for similar reasons.[2]

China has recently revived its campaign in hopes that some of
the political opposition to its WTO membership will evaporate
after the 1996 U.S. presidential elections. Chinese officials have
been making the case for Chinese membership in the WTO
around the world. As part of this campaign, Assistant Minister of
MOFTEC Long Yongtu visited the United States and made a
two-part argument on why China must be admitted to the WTO
as soon as possible.[3] First, he noted that China would soon be the
largest economy in the world and that the world trading system

would lose credibility if China were not a member. Second, he argued that when Chinese ministries were in dispute over whether to abide by WTO provisions or adopt a mercantilist policy, the mercantilists won because China was not yet a WTO member.

These arguments have some weaknesses, but they also hold kernels of truth. China's economic size and its increasing trade success are strong reasons to include it in the WTO. The credibility of the WTO as a trade policeman would be damaged much more severely, however, if China were allowed to join without being forced to conform to the rules of the WTO. Further, Long's analysis fails to note that China's credibility is also at stake. As long as China is not in the WTO, it remains a second-class citizen in the trading system and is denied the secure export markets that WTO membership would provide. Long's second argument is, of course, at the core of the reason that many western countries support China's membership. The unanswered question in Long's scenario, however, is, Would WTO membership be enough to tilt policy decisions against the mercantilists? This is the central question in the debate over Chinese WTO membership.

**The Western Perspective**

From a western perspective, the main reason to admit China to the WTO is simple: it would obligate China, at least in theory, to abandon many of its mercantilist trade policies. The driving concern here is to avoid a repeat of the Japan experience, in which a country became a successful exporter while practicing protectionism at home.[4] Whether China has more or fewer trade barriers than Japan did twenty years ago is an ultimately unanswerable question. It depends how one determines the overall level of protection. The question is also of limited relevance. China is without a doubt a highly protected market and is pursuing policies that are, in many ways, incompatible with free trade and free markets.

If China's economy could be made more open to trade and

compatible with the principles of free trade, it would be a significant positive development for both China and the rest of the world. The Chinese people would benefit from an increased selection of products; consumers around the world would have access to Chinese products; and global growth would gain a significant boost. As the next chapter will explain, mere membership in the WTO may not be enough to achieve these goals, but few would disagree on their desirability.

The most tangible and obvious benefit to other WTO members would be increased exports to China. If China's trade barriers were only tariffs, and if there were more experience with the Chinese market, economists could give a solid estimate of the amount that exports would likely increase. Such an estimate is impossible, however, for several reasons. First and foremost, it is impossible to predict which Chinese trade barriers might be lowered in a WTO accession agreement and what kind of barriers might remain. For example, what would be the effect if all tariffs were eliminated but the Chinese government continued to manage "demand" for imports. The effect might be great or it might be almost nonexistent, depending upon the decisions of the Chinese government.

Further, it is difficult to predict how Chinese consumers, both individual and industrial, might initially react to increased availability of imports. It is possible that due to rising nationalism or limited foreign exchange they would still shun imports. It is also possible that imported products would be very appealing to consumers.

The most that can be done is to generate some order-of-magnitude estimates of the impact of China's increasing its propensity to import. Given the level of Chinese trade barriers and the pace of growth in China, it is entirely possible that China's propensity to import could increase by 20 percent or even 30 percent over a period of years as trade barriers are lowered. A 30 percent increase in import propensity by 2005, for example, could result in $86 billion in additional global exports to China, and an extra $10 billion in U.S. exports in that year alone.

Given the U.S. Commerce Department's rule of thumb that a

$1 billion increase in exports creates 17,000 new jobs, export increases of this magnitude would be politically as well as economically significant.

Obviously, all of these estimates are highly speculative, but given the nature of the problem of trying to predict increases in Chinese exports, rough estimates are probably the best that can be made. And, at the very least, they demonstrate that the direct economic stakes are considerable.

### Avoiding a New Japan

The rationale for controlling Chinese protectionism, however, goes beyond simply opening new Chinese markets for western goods. Among the most significant developments in the economic history of the later half of the twentieth century is the rise of a new generation of Asian mercantilist economies, typified by Japan and South Korea. A full description of this history is beyond the scope of this discussion and is available from a number of other sources.[5]

In brief, however, in order to rebuild its economy after World War II, Japan adopted a modern version of mercantilism. The usual pattern has involved developing pivotal manufacturing industries, including autos and semiconductors, through a staged process that included government aid in developing these manufacturing industries, trade protection to create a secure home market, and, finally, an export campaign to turn the new industries into world leaders while generating export revenues.[6]

South Korea has followed essentially the same strategy, focusing its efforts on many of the same industries originally targeted for development by Japan—steel, semiconductors, and, more recently, automobiles. Even South Korea's economic critics concede that its efforts have been generally successful. South Korea has become a world-class steel producer and has made impressive strides in the manufacture of both semiconductors and automobiles.[7]

Viewed from the perspective of the world economy, particularly Japan's and South Korea's trading partners, these programs have been quite costly. In pure economic terms, they have distorted comparative advantage in the industries in which they operate, resulting in a net economic loss worldwide. In more concrete terms, the rise of Asian industrial policy has cost western economies, particularly the United States, both industries and employment. This has particularly been the case in heavy industries, such as steel. A number of other sophisticated manufacturing sectors, such as automobiles and semiconductors, also experienced significant competitive setbacks as a result of these industrial policies, though they have recovered somewhat in subsequent years.[8]

*Will China Follow the Pattern?*

As the previous section noted, there are strong indications that China is intent on building industrial strength using a pattern pioneered by Japan and South Korea. Even without any of the documentation mentioned earlier, it is difficult to believe that China would not at least attempt to follow this same pattern. After all, the stated goal of China's economic planners is rapid development of a strong industrial base in advanced industries. That being the case, how could China's economic planners ignore the meteoric rise of Japan and South Korea?

Again, this is not to say that China is identical to Japan and South Korea. They are different countries with significant economic, historical, political, and cultural distinctions. Nonetheless, any reasonable individual given the task of rapidly nurturing industries would look to recent successes for indications of how to proceed. In the last thirty years, Japan and South Korea provide those successful examples.

Taiwan, "the other China," has also pursued industrial policy with considerable success. Taiwan's success has helped it build a strong industrial base, which has allowed it to grow rapidly and greatly improve the standard of living of its citizens. As most readers are likely aware, Taiwan's historical roots run back to the nationalists that were driven from the mainland after the communist revolution in 1948. The economic rise of Taiwan has allowed it to grow into a sizable world economic power and to retain its independence from the mainland. Taiwan's economic success is certainly a political thorn in the side of Beijing, but it also drives home the reality that industrial policy can work.[9]

### Is There Cause for Concern?

If China is allowed to develop a new permutation of Asian industrial policy, one that takes advantage of the influx of outside investment, western industries are likely to be buffeted by a new generation of government-sponsored competitors.

Some commentators will likely argue that this is not cause for too much concern. After all, the United States and other western economies survived the rise of Japan and South Korea, and consumers have benefited from a greater selection of products. In the end, their argument goes, those who distort trade really hurt themselves more than their trading partners. Although this position can be defended within the confines of an economics textbook, it ignores many political and economic realities.[10]

A Chinese industrial policy would likely again lead to comparative advantage being distorted on a large scale. The Japanese and South Korean industries spawned by industrial policy have not withered on the vine; they remain strong and powerful competitive industries. Employing a concept known as strategic trade theory, many economists now suggest that the positive "spillover effects" for other industries actually make these industrial policies defensible. Some even use this as a rationale for the United States to pursue a similar policy.[11]

Whatever the outcome of that debate, however, there are predictable direct effects. Western industries will lose sales and workers will be laid off. Governments will experience significant costs in increased unemployment benefits and lost tax revenues. In theory, these adjustment costs should be transient and will disappear once the displaced workers and other resources shift to other industries.

This shift, however, assumes such things as full employment, no entry costs, and so forth. These assumptions may be defensible on a blackboard, but they are very questionable in the real world. This perhaps is why no government in history has adopted this laissez faire outlook in making its trade and economic policy. Far more common is one that expends great effort to nurture manufacturing industries and capture the employment they create.

Of course, there are also political implications to be considered in this discussion. Even if the arguments of laissez faire economics are accepted, recent political events, such as the 1996 U.S. presidential campaign, demonstrate that these views are not widely accepted by American voters and politicians. Republican candidate Pat Buchanan made significant headway in advocating protectionism. All other major candidates advocated an aggressive trade policy to counter foreign industrial policies and trade barriers.

Other western democracies have been even less accepting of unilateral free trade than the United States. European politicians took a number of steps to limit Japanese imports and currently impose quotas on Chinese products.[12]

If Chinese industrial policy were to result in displacements rivaling those caused by Japan's earlier policy, a political response is nearly certain. Japan's industrial policy went without response because the United States was confident in its economic strength after World War II and Japan was not seen as an economic threat. As just mentioned, a much different political environment exists today. A strong political response, which could include a surge of protectionism and even the destruction of the trading system, is possible. This could lead to a decrease in economic opportunities and growth worldwide.

Despite the views of some academics, reciprocal free trade is the only liberal economic philosophy that appears politically viable. If China is unwilling to seek a reciprocal trading and economic relationship, serious and very negative political and economic consequences are almost certain to result.

*Forewarned Is Forearmed?*

What, then, is the western world, particularly the United States, to do? Simply wait for the inevitable economic fallout or is there some way to head off economic problems? Essentially, there are three choices. First, the United States could follow the advice of laissez faire economists and do nothing. For reasons just outlined, this is not viable.

Second, the United States could pursue selective protectionism against China to control the impact of Chinese mercantilism upon the U.S. economy. This is essentially what Europe has done by imposing quotas on Chinese products. Arguably, it is also the effect of U.S. antidumping duties.

Selected protection or, at least, the threat of trade sanctions will likely be a necessary element of any effective policy, but such an approach has two serious limitations. First, it does not get to the heart of the problem: Chinese mercantilism. It merely addresses a symptom, albeit a major one, but a symptom nonetheless. Second, in addition to potential losses in consumer welfare, such an approach has costs for the United States. It would tend to increase tension between Washington, as the capital of China's leading market, and Beijing. This could limit U.S. access to the growing Chinese market and potentially spark wider conflicts.

The third and most attractive option, however, is to use the process of integrating China into the WTO to curb Chinese mercantilism, of which industrial policy is one major element. Today's WTO has stronger dispute settlement procedures and substantive provisions than the GATT as it existed when Japan and Korea launched their efforts at industrial policy. If the WTO had been in place and its members had chosen to use its provisions, it could likely have blocked Japan's industrial policy efforts.

If China were forced to abide by the terms of the WTO, then at least the worst aspects of current mercantilist policies could be curbed. Three particular provisions of the WTO could be important in this regard. First, the WTO's general prohibitions against nontariff barriers could open the Chinese market. In particular, if

China were forced to commit to significant market opening in the WTO accession process, it would be practically impossible for China to follow Japan's pattern of protectionism at home to create a secure home market in which to nurture targeted industries.

Second, the WTO's new investment code, known as the Agreement on Trade Related Investment Measures, or TRIMs, could provide a check on China's investment performance requirements. As discussed in the previous section, these performance requirements are already a serious trade distortion responsible in large part for China's global trade surplus and its large surplus with the United States. In the longer term, performance requirements have the potential to distort comparative advantage and create competitors for U.S. and other western manufacturing industries.

The TRIMs provisions of the WTO were literally designed to combat just such a problem. The core principle of TRIMs is national treatment, which, in simple terms, means that foreign investments must be treated the same as domestic entities. The TRIMs agreement would rule out requirements that foreign investments export a fixed percentage of production, maintain a foreign exchange balance, or transfer technology. Export requirements and foreign exchange balancing requirements are actually included on an illustrative list of prohibited practices.[13]

A third feature of the WTO that could curb some of China's mercantilist practices is the new agreement on subsidies. As discussed in the previous section, the WTO has a much stronger antisubsidy provision than the GATT. The WTO creates a new category of subsidies that are presumed to violate the WTO and are to be treated with serious prejudice; the category includes subsidies accounting for more than 5 percent of the value of products, subsidies to cover operating losses of a firm or industry, and debt forgiveness.[14] China's current state aid to SOEs would likely violate each of these three tests. Further, the ongoing subsidies of energy, labor, and raw materials would likely render many non-SOE enterprises vulnerable to subsidy complaints under the WTO.

Under the GATT, the primary remedy for subsidies were offsetting or countervailing duties. Countervailing duties are still available under the WTO, but serious prejudice subsidies are prohibited and subject to dispute settlement action. If a country operated a serious prejudice subsidy, it would not only open the products produced under such subsidy schemes vulnerable to countervailing duties, it would also be vulnerable to losing a WTO dispute settlement case and be subject to trade retaliation.[15]

Other WTO provisions on a range of topics would also limit China's current mercantilist policies and make it very difficult for it to continue a Japan-style industrial policy. In fact, if the WTO provisions are enforced, China will have to undertake sweeping economic reforms, forcing it to adopt a true market economic system.

Successfully curbing China's industrial policy/mercantilistic ambitions with the WTO would also send a powerful message to other countries that might be inclined to follow the Japanese model, particularly in Asia and Eastern Europe. Thus, the effective handling of China's integration into the WTO has the potential to close the door permanently on Japan copycats.

### Ending Communism

As a full-fledged economic competitor to capitalism, communism has been a dead ideology for nearly a decade. The epic struggle did not end because of military superiority or victory on the battlefield, although the former may have hastened the decline of the Soviet Union. It ended because the success of the capitalist system in spurring economic growth and development, and improving the quality of life of those living under it proved too compelling an example to resist. Even the countries that remain nominally communist, such as China, Vietnam, North Korea, and Cuba, have essentially admitted defeat and begun to experiment with market economics.

As with China, however, the transition is not complete. Each of the countries mentioned remains somewhere on the continuum between communist economics and market economics. Although there is still a long way to go, China, Russia, and some of the former Soviet republics have made substantial progress in this transition. Vietnam is undertaking a rapid reform process to move in the market direction.[16] North Korea and Cuba lag behind and their citizens pay the price.[17] Nonetheless, in the coming decades there can be little doubt that these once state-run economies will continue the transition toward market economics and seek to become more fully integrated into the world economy.

Many of the most serious problems to be faced as China is integrated into the WTO involve addressing the many holdovers of communism that are simply incompatible with the market trading system, including state-directed industrial plans and government support of SOEs. These challenges will be confronted again and again as Russia, Vietnam, and other formerly communist countries follow China's lead and seek WTO membership. Thus, the task of integrating China into the WTO should be viewed as creating the template that will be followed with a long list of other countries in the coming decades.

Of course, the full integration of these nonmarket economies into the market trading system is of tremendous historic importance. In a sense, it is a sort of reconstruction plan for the end of the Cold War. If China's integration into the WTO is handled smoothly, a whole range of potential economic and political problems can be headed off and the struggle between communism and capitalism can truly be brought to an end. By the same token, this task cannot be handled through quick political fixes. Chinese integration into the WTO will set the pattern for the world economy in the post–Cold War world, not a challenge to be addressed with a quick, politically inspired deal.

### Hong Kong and Taiwan

Beyond the enormous political and economic stakes just outlined, there are two practical reasons to move forward with China's membership. These problems involve the two other Chinas—Hong Kong and Taiwan.

Hong Kong is a nearly unique pseudo-state. It is a tiny enclave on China's border that China leased to Great Britain in another era on a ninety-nine-year lease. While under the control of Great Britain, tiny Hong Kong grew into a world financial center and the port through which most of China's trade with the world flowed. Hong Kong is also the base from which many western companies operate their holdings within China. Hong Kong adopted the British notions of free trade and has been a member in good standing of the GATT since 1986.[18]

Hong Kong's status in the trading system, however, is about to become complicated. Hong Kong will remain a WTO member, but the ninety-nine-year lease is up and control of Hong Kong will pass from London to Beijing in the summer of 1997.[19] If China is still not a WTO member, this will create a remarkably awkward situation in which Hong Kong would be in the WTO even though the sovereign power controlling it would not. This will certainly weigh on Chinese national pride.

The practical implications, however, raise even greater concerns. China had pledged to allow Hong Kong to continue as it is with no interference from Beijing, but with nearly each passing month, China takes some action to call that pledge into question. As discussed in Chapter 5, China has already shipped textiles through Hong Kong to circumvent international agreements and national trade laws. If China remains outside the WTO, the potential for its using Hong Kong to circumvent national laws and gain indirect WTO membership would be enormous.

The "Hong Kong situation" can be handled in several ways. If China remains outside the WTO, the burden will fall to national customs authorities to exercise greater scrutiny of trade with Hong Kong. With Hong Kong in Chinese hands and Hong Kong authorities cooperating with China, this could prove a very difficult task. The simplest and ultimate solution would be to bring China into the WTO. Given the complex issues that need to be addressed, however, this may well prove impossible by the summer of 1997.

The problem related to Taiwan is very different but no less complex. As noted, Taiwan is the home of the nationalist Chinese who fled the mainland after the communist revolution. Even then, there were GATT implications to the plight of the nationalist Chinese. In 1948, nationalist China became an original GATT member. In 1950, however, to deny the benefits of GATT membership to the communists, nationalist China withdrew from the GATT.[20] Since the communists were already in control of China, a legitimate question could be raised as to the appropriateness of nationalist China being allowed to take such a step. The People's Republic of China was initially little interested in trade with the West, however, and did not fight the withdrawal.

In the mid-1960s, trade became increasingly important to Taiwan and it sought and was granted observer status in the GATT. When the West recognized communist China in the early 1970s, however, it was forced to derecognize Taiwan since both claimed to be the legitimate government of China. As a result, Taiwan lost its observer status in 1971.[21]

Taiwan became an increasingly powerful trading country in the intervening years. When China formally sought membership in the GATT in 1987, Taiwan also began an effort to win membership. Because there can only be one government of China, Taiwan was forced to apply for membership in 1990 as the customs territory of Chinese Taipei. Taiwan's application was accepted for consideration and a working party was appointed to consider it.[22] Although it had a protectionist history, Taiwan shed many of its trade barriers and offered to shed more in an agreement to join the GATT. Many western countries were impressed with the quality of Taiwan's application for membership.

The complex politics between China and Taiwan once again intervened, however. China did not want Taiwan's application to proceed faster than its own, even though Taiwan's economy and trading system were much more developed and it was a much stronger candidate for GATT membership. The issue was a point of national pride for China. Acting through sympathetic GATT members, China has been able to hold up Taiwan's application at least until China is granted membership.[23]

This situation solves China's political problems, but it is unsatisfactory from an economic perspective. The island of Taiwan is already the world's thirteenth largest trading country. From the perspective of the United States, Taiwan is also a bigger market. With a small fraction of the population and territory, Taiwan imported almost twice as much from the United States in 1995 as China.[24] If Taiwan were forced to open its market as part of a WTO accession agreement, additional export opportunities would be created for the United States and other trading countries.

If China is allowed to enter the WTO, the Chinese have pledged to allow Taiwan to enter as well. Most WTO members, including the United States and the EU, seem satisfied with this general formula for membership. Thus, in this matter and many others, the fate of mainland China and Taiwan are joined.

## The Chinese Perspective

Potentially, the West has a considerable amount to gain from China's entering the WTO. It is, however, China that sought membership in 1987 and it is China that continues to press for membership. Given the significant reforms that China would be forced to undertake in order to join the WTO, China's enthusiasm for membership is, at least superficially, surprising. In fact, when China first sought membership in the world trading system it was probably driven by national pride. The logic was simple—China was a great nation and deserved membership in global institutions, including the WTO. Beyond that, there are three reasons why China continues to seek WTO membership.

First, national pride is still a major force. China is not only a great nation now, but a trading power—the world's tenth largest exporter. It is this national pride that seems to drive statements by Chinese officials that the WTO cannot be a credible world trade organization if China is excluded. The continuing prospect that Taiwan might somehow win membership in the WTO before China, if China's membership campaign were to stall, also drives China forward. It would be yet another serious blow to Chinese pride if the nationalists, driven to a small island after the revolution, were to be recognized as having built a more advanced economy than mainland China.

A second factor that seems to drive China are economic reformers within China. Despite the vestiges of communism in the Chinese economy, there is a strong political force advocating economic reform. Although there is still far to go, reformers have won more policy battles in the last decade than they have lost. Still, there is a continuing struggle over economic policy. It appears that some advocates of reform believe that WTO membership could "lock in" economic reforms and set the course for further reforms. Certainly, those Chinese who make this argument do so partly for western consumption, but there does seem to be some truth to it.

Finally, the primary and most important motivation for China's efforts to join the WTO is to secure market access for Chinese exports. Exports remain a primary ingredient of China's strategy to develop its economy. Currently, other countries are not obligated to continue to offer China market access for their exports, though they do so voluntarily. At least in theory, any of China's export markets could decide to impose prohibitive tariffs or quotas on Chinese goods and violate no international agreement, except possibly bilateral understandings with China that lack dispute settlement procedures and carry limited weight. Of course, there would likely be consequences to such a decision. China has a number of options for exerting economic and political influence. Still, WTO membership would provide another strong protection and give China some additional assurance of access to export markets. A country as dependent on exports for growth as China naturally seeks maximum protection for its market access.

The most serious problem for China in this regard has been the United States. A Cold War–era law known as the Jackson–Vanik Amendment requires that most-favored-nation (MFN) trading status be provided to China on a conditional basis with the status reviewed each year. MFN is somewhat of a misnomer since almost all U.S. trading partners enjoy MFN; if MFN were denied China, Chinese exports would be faced with prohibitive tariffs, and the majority of Chinese exports to the United States and perhaps as much as 90 percent of total Sino-U.S. trade would be halted.[25]

Originally, Jackson–Vanik was aimed at encouraging the Soviet Union and its Eastern European satellites to allow emigration of religious minorities. China was included in the statute but was not the focus of any real debate or discussion. After Tiananmen Square, however, congressional human rights advocates seized upon Jackson–Vanik as a way to punish China for its abuses of human rights. Every year since 1989, there has been a debate with some in Congress advocating withdrawal of MFN status from China for a long list of grievances. Given the disruptive impact upon trade and the likelihood that MFN status withdrawal would not change Chinese human rights policy, Congress has never actually withdrawn China's MFN status, and an increasing majority seems to favor continuing MFN. Still, the annual ritual, however lacking in credibility, continues.[26]

Chinese officials will volunteer that one of the primary objectives behind the 1987 application to join the world trading system was to block the operation of Jackson–Vanik. Apparently, the Chinese realized that Jackson–Vanik could become a problem even before it became the focus of U.S. congressional attention. The Chinese seem to have overlooked the fact that GATT/WTO membership, by itself, would not render Jackson–Vanik ineffective. The GATT and the WTO both contain nonapplication provisions, which allow one member to refuse to extend the benefits of membership to another. If so inclined, the United States could allow China to become a WTO member but assert a nonapplication exception and continue to apply Jackson–Vanik to China.

Jackson–Vanik does, however, provide the United States with a bargaining chip to use in negotiations with China. The United States could hold out the prospect of repealing Jackson–Vanik or exempting China in order to win additional concessions from China in WTO accession negotiations. The credibility of this strategy is somewhat limited because the U.S. Congress seems increasingly inclined to extend MFN status, but that could always change if the political winds shift or if events spark a renewed focus upon China. Thus, although Jackson–Vanik has outlived its original purpose, it could find a new, useful purpose in connection with China.

## Conclusion

The elements of an agreement on China's joining the WTO appear to be in place. The West has good reason for seeking to integrate China into the world economy beginning with the WTO, and China shares the goal albeit for a different set of reasons.

Unfortunately, it is not quite as simple as that. Joining the WTO, for example, means very different things to the West and to China. To the West, it means forcing China to drop the trappings of Marxism and protectionism and engage in free and open trade. To China, it means securing markets but not necessarily engaging in further economic reforms. These differences in goals and definitions of WTO membership can only be worked out through a difficult, issue-by-issue negotiation for which neither side has yet shown itself prepared.

The many roadblocks to China's WTO membership are discussed in the next chapter, and those roadblocks are daunting. The problems cannot be addressed overnight, and any effort to forge a quick political deal will likely create more problems than it solves. Still, the elements for one of the most significant economic and trade agreements ever struck are in place; there is a historic opportunity.

## Notes

1. For a useful timeline of these events, see Nicholas R. Lardy, *China in the World Economy* (Washington, DC: Institute for International Economics, 1994), 141–43.

2. Greg Mastel, *China and the WTO: Economy at the Crossroad* (Washington, DC: The Economic Strategy Institute, 1994).

3. Todd Crowell, David Hsieh, and Sam Gilston, "A New Maturity? Amid a Flurry of Activity, America and China Prepare to Move Their Troubled Ties onto a Higher Plane," *Asiaweek,* November 8, 1996.

4. Chalmers Johnson, *Japan: Who Governs?* (New York: W.W. Norton, 1995).

5. Ibid.; and Danny M. Leipziger and Peter A. Petri, *Korean Industrial*

*Policy,* a World Bank discussion paper (Washington, DC: The World Bank, 1993).

6. Ibid.

7. Ibid.

8. Thomas R. Howell, William A. Noellert, Jesse G. Krier, and Alan Wm. Wolff, *Steel and the State* (Boulder, CO: Westview Press, 1988); and Clyde Prestowitz, *Trading Places: How We Allowed Japan to Take the Lead* (New York: Basic Books, 1988).

9. Dick Kirschten, "The Other China," *National Journal,* October 8, 1994, 2332–34.

10. For some examples from this viewpoint, see Jagdish N. Bagwati and Robert E. Hudec, eds., *Fair Trade and Harmonization: Prerequisites for Free Trade?* (Cambridge, MA: MIT Press, 1996).

11. Laura D'Andrea Tyson, *Who's Bashing Whom?* (Washington, DC: Institute for International Economics, 1992).

12. Elizabeth Pisani, "EU Comes Courting with Vows of Support," *Asia Times,* November 14, 1996.

13. *Final Texts of the GATT Uruguay Round Agreements Including the Agreement Establishing the World Trade Organization,* Agreement on Trade Related Investment Measures, Annex, April 15, 1994.

14. Ibid., Agreement on Subsidies and Countervailing Measures, Articles 5 and 6.

15. Ibid.

16. Daniel Pruzin, "Vietnam's Communists Feud on Pace of Reform," *Christian Science Monitor,* July 2, 1996.

17. Yoshitoshi Sasaki, "U.S. Should Lighten Up on Cuba Issue," *Daily Yomiuri,* May 29, 1996; and David Holley, "Politics Could Impact North Korean Famine," *Houston Chronicle,* December 30, 1995.

18. Lardy, *China in the World Economy,* 141–43.

19. Greg Mastel, "Three Chinas and the WTO," *Journal of Commerce,* August 9, 1996.

20. A discussion of these events can be found in Harold K. Jacobson and Michel Oksenberg, *China's Participation in the IMF, the World Bank, and the GATT: Toward a Global Economic Order* (Ann Arbor: University of Michigan Press, 1990).

21. Ibid.; and Lardy, *China in the World Economy,* 141–43.

22. Ibid.; and John Zarcostas, "West Upbeat on Taiwan Talks, Doubtful on China Progress," *Journal of Commerce,* July 26, 1993.

23. Ibid.

24. U.S. Department of Commerce, trade statistics, 1995.

25. U.S.-China Business Council, *The Implication of Denying China MFN Status* (Self-published monograph, 1996).

26. For some examples of press coverage on this topic, see Richard Grenier, "Trade and Other Wars with China," *Washington Times,* March 21, 1994; and John M. Marshall, "China Weighing the Benefits of Trade," *San Francisco Chronicle,* May 16, 1994.

# 10

## Good Ideas in Good Time

China's efforts to join the GATT were formally launched in July 1986,[1] but China's campaign has not been consistent. It picked up urgency in 1994 and 1995 when the GATT was being replaced by the WTO.[2] China sought to become a founding member of the WTO, but this effort failed because China was not willing to commit to sufficient reforms in order to win membership. Several smaller campaigns for WTO membership have been launched by the Chinese, but they tend to focus on winning international support with little attention to the necessary economic reforms.

For their part, western countries have also been somewhat remiss. In the late 1980s and early 1990s, the United States, in particular, seemed to view membership for China in the world trading system as unrealistic. This view seemed based largely upon congressional opposition to granting China any favors in the immediate aftermath of Tiananmen Square, not upon an assessment of the economic task involved. In recent years, the United States, the European Union, Japan, and other WTO members have given serious consideration to the task of integrating China into the world system. A number of WTO working party meetings have been held, and many countries have had bilateral consultations with China on specific concerns.[3] Many of the documents produced by the United States and Europe in particular are well thought out and contain innovative concepts.[4] These positions are discussed in more detail in the next chapter.

Still, outside forces such as congressional politics, presidential campaigns, and diplomatic initiatives have often intervened to mix the message and push this work into the background. These mixed messages from the West have likely contributed to China's apparent belief that WTO membership can be won by "winning friends internationally" without serious economic reforms.

It sometimes seems that neither side recognizes the enormity of the task at hand. The negotiation over WTO membership involves nothing less than integrating the last great nonmarket economy in the market trading system. As stressed in the previous chapter, these negotiations are of enormous economic and political significance. In addition to the enormous significance of WTO membership for China, this is probably a first step in integrating China into other multilateral institutions.[5] Given the range of issues that must be addressed and the political will required from both sides, the negotiations on WTO membership will probably take some time. The full integration of China into the world economy will take much longer still, but the potential payoffs make all these efforts worthwhile.

With every great opportunity come great risks and this is no exception. A literal minefield of issues face negotiators, and there is constant political pressure for a quick deal. If these issues are mishandled in order to rush an agreement for a summit or other political event, most of the potential benefits could disappear and new problems could be created.

To more fully explore these topics, this chapter will focus upon some of the key issues that must be addressed. It will also discuss interim measures that can serve to diffuse problems until a final agreement is reached.

## Developing Country Status

In one limited sense, the comment that neither side has recognized the enormity of the task at hand is incorrect. In its initial offer during WTO accession negotiations, China argued that it would take many years to phase in WTO discipline.[6] China seeks to gain the most lenient treatment allowable under the WTO. The

Chinese likely knew this and made the offer to emphasize two points. First, they were simply employing good bargaining strategy in seeking to negotiate an accession agreement with as long a phase-in or transition period as possible. Second, and in a related vein, the Chinese were using this century-long phase-in proposal to dramatize their position that China should be treated as a developing country by the WTO.

The issue of developing country status for China is probably the most difficult in China's WTO negotiations, and its resolution could affect many other issues. On its face, China's demand for developing country status seems quite reasonable. By the normal definitions of the term, China is a developing country. Although its exact level is open to debate, China's per capita income is still quite low. Despite the economic progress in the coastal provinces, China's interior provinces still suffer from crushing poverty and a lack of economic development. China is the leading recipient of developmental lending from the World Bank.[7]

To understand developing country status and the issues it raises, however, it is necessary to go back to the very beginnings of the multilateral trading system. The United States was the initial driving force behind the world trading system. In the immediate postwar era, the United States was the only major economic power not devastated by World War II; this gave the United States an enormous economic edge over the rest of the world. Further, the Cold War struggle between capitalism and communism under the de facto leadership of the United States and the Soviet Union was already taking shape. As a result, the United States simultaneously sought to bolster the capitalist system and draw additional countries to its economic viewpoint. Pursuing this goal, the United States demonstrated enormous economic generosity with programs like the Marshall Plan.

The establishment of the world trading system created an opportunity to advance both of the United States' goals. First, by expanding trade among western countries, a tremendous engine for growth was unleashed in market-oriented countries. Second, trade could be used to transfer even more wealth to other recovering and emerging market countries than aid. Poorer developing countries were granted "special and differential treatment." In the parlance of the trading system, this meant that developing countries were granted secure access to developed markets but were exempted from many GATT disciplines and allowed to keep their markets closed; this practice is often referred to as free-riding on the trading system. In the GATT, countries were even allowed to self-elect or determine for themselves if they should be treated as developing countries.[8]

Initially, this status was sought by poorer countries like Cuba, which argued that temporary protection was necessary to allow the development of their manufacturing base. At the time, this line of argument was supported by a line of economic thinking known as infant industry theory. The infant industry doctrine holds that trade protection should be permissible for purposes of allowing new industries to get their start.[9]

As an economic doctrine, infant industry theory is now widely discredited. In theory, of course, trade barriers almost always result in a net economic loss. The infant industry theory, however, has some particular problems. Foremost among them, many of the countries that have pursued it, notably India and Brazil, have generally made themselves poorer and failed to nurture new industries.[10] Ironically, both of these countries have begun to grow stronger and develop new industries now that they have abandoned some of their previous protectionism. To further support the point, the developing countries that have made the most dramatic strides forward, like Singapore and Hong Kong, have pursued liberal trading policies and kept their markets open.[11]

As noted in the previous chapter, some economists have even adopted a related theory that holds that positive "spillover effects" on other industries and the economy in general sometimes justify protection, but this theory speaks to nurturing emerging high-tech industries in which the technology is just developing.[12] It is not a modern "infant industry" notion.

In a similar vein, however, the success of Japan and Korea could provide a stronger modern argument for infant industry.

The weakness in this position, however, is that the success of Japanese and Korean efforts had as much or more to do with targeting of export markets as domestic protectionism. Further, even if Japanese and Korean successes can be cited in support of infant industry policies for the country pursuing them, these policies have also distorted trade patterns, created trade conflicts, and, if continued, will likely destroy the political consensus for free trade on which the global trading system depends. The net economic loss resulting from a collapse of the system and a possible resurgence of protectionism would be incalculable.[13]

In short, the economic underpinnings of the concept of developing country status are very questionable. The political history that allowed the status to be created is bound to a unique window in history and no longer exists. "Special and differential" treatment has been widely abused by economic powerhouses, such as Korea, that have attempted to assert this status even after their industrial base was well established.[14]

All of these developments have led to the calling into question of the very concept of special and differential treatment. In fact, the United States made eliminating freeriders on the trading system a primary objective in the Uruguay Round negotiations, which established the WTO. The United States achieved some notable progress in this regard by eliminating the "voluntary" aspects of some multilateral trade agreements or codes under the GATT rubric and by tightening some other provisions that had been abused by freeriders. Nonetheless, the concept continues to play a role in the WTO.[15]

China's effort to employ developing country status illustrates why the concept has the potential to create serious trade problems. It is important first to note that the term *developing country status* means something very different in the context of the global trading system than it does in the context of the World Bank. China's per capita income is low enough to qualify it for developing country status for the purposes of the World Bank and other international development programs, but in the context of the GATT/WTO the term refers to the strength of the country's industrial base and its ability to compete in international markets. Without repeating too many statistics brought to bear earlier in the discussion, it is worth repeating that China has enjoyed almost unprecedented industrial development in the last decade. China's exports have grown at three times the world average for two decades; it is already one of the world's top ten exporters.[16] Further, China is hardly forced to export only agricultural and natural resource products; in fact, Chinese exports have as high a manufactured product content as U.S. exports.[17] This is not to say that China's industries are fully developed; they are not. If China is, however, allowed to take advantage of special protections to build its industries, virtually every other country should be allowed to exploit those special protections. Were this the case, the exceptions would soon overpower the rule and the world trading system would cease to provide any discipline of trade.

In practical terms, if China is allowed to exploit developing country status as it has requested, many of the benefits of bringing China into the WTO discussed in the last chapter would fail to materialize. Despite the efforts of the United States and other major trading countries, the WTO still includes many special treatments for "least developed countries"—the category China seeks to join. The WTO includes a separate decision statement acknowledging that least developed countries will still receive special and differential treatment. The special understandings extended to the countries in this category include more time to submit liberalization schedules, ability to maintain trade barriers to meet balance-of-payments objectives, special treatment under intellectual property provisions, special exemptions from government procurement provision, and so on.[18]

As the listing of barriers in Part II made clear, China could exploit these provisions to continue piracy of intellectual property,[19] keep government procurement markets closed,[20] and generally continue to practice protectionism. The special treatment granted to least developed countries regarding subsidies[21] and trade-related investment measures (TRIMs)[22] deserves special mention.

As discussed in the previous chapter, WTO discipline on subsidies would force real change in the Chinese economic system. Subsidies are an integral part of the SOE programs and extend throughout the Chinese economy. The subsidy discipline would effectively remove an important Chinese tool for mercantilism. In this agreement as in others, however, developing countries are granted special treatment. Developing countries are generally granted eight years to phase out subsidies, with some shorter time limits on export subsidies.[23] Least developed countries, as China wishes to be considered, are largely exempted from new subsidy discipline.[24]

Given the integral role that subsidies play in the Chinese system, it is probably reasonable that China be given some special considerations as to the phase-out of subsidy programs. All developing countries have an eight-year phase-out period, however. Beyond that, Article 29 of the subsidy agreement grants that: "Members in the process of transformation from a centrally planned into a market, free-enterprise economy may apply programmes and measures necessary for such a transformation."[25] Going beyond that and allowing one of the largest economies in the world to subsidize at will for as long as it wishes would seriously undermine the purpose of the entire subsidy agreement —disciplining one of the most significant remaining trade-distorting practices.

As also discussed previously, the TRIMs agreement has the potential to control perhaps the most worrisome Chinese trade distortion, investment performance requirements. Article 4 of the TRIMs agreement, however, grants a near exemption from the provisions of the agreement to developing countries.[26] If China were able to enter the WTO with developing country status, the TRIMs provisions would have little effect.

Given its economic status, China should legitimately be granted some special considerations concerning the phase-in periods for certain disciplines. As a practical matter, that is already agreed to by all parties. In some areas, however, China should require no special considerations at all. China's bilateral agreements with the United States and the European Union on protection of intellectual property already obligate China to provide a level of intellectual property protection beyond that required by the WTO.[27]

Most importantly, it is simply not economically warranted or politically acceptable to have one of the world's most successful trading economies granted membership in the WTO on what amounts to a special dispensation that would allow it to gain all of the benefits while shirking most of the responsibilities. Such an arrangement would transform China into a gigantic freerider on the trading system, and it is unlikely the system could carry such a burden. China's manufacturing industries are world powers, not infants, and they do not deserve the special protections intended for infant industries.

Obviously, the issue of whether or not China is granted developing country status is of enormous practical importance. Given the nature of accession negotiations, however, this will not likely be a yes or no decision. Through the accession negotiations, it is possible to tailor exactly which disciplines China will be bound to and which disciplines it will phase in over time. Thus, it is entirely possible to negotiate an arrangement that is sensitive to China's legitimate concerns while still obligating China to observe WTO principles, at least after a phase-in period. Such an approach is far superior to simply granting China the blank check of special and differential treatment.[28]

## China as a Precedent

The direct benefits of curbing China's mercantilism are numerous. A vast new export market would be opened, China would be blocked from following the path blazed by Japan, and true economic reform and an end to communism could be encouraged in China and other nonmarket economies. All of this could be a boon to China's consumers, its trading partners, and ultimately the world economy.

China's WTO accession negotiations have another important function. Most of the world's countries are members of the WTO, but there are still important nonmembers. As discussed in the

Table 10.1

**GDP of Various Countries Seeking WTO Membership, 1994**
($PPP billions)

| Country or region | GDP |
| --- | --- |
| Baltics | 31.8 |
| Belarus | 47.1 |
| Caucasus | 24.5 |
| Central Asia | 75.4 |
| Kazakhstan | 40.5 |
| Moldova | 8.8 |
| Russia | 618.1 |
| Ukraine | 154.4 |
| Vietnam | 83.5 |
| Saudi Arabia | 187.0 |
| China | 3,021.5 |
| Taiwan | 274.0 |
| Total | 4,566.6 |
| Total (low China est.) | 3,811.1 |

*Source:* DRI/McGraw Hill, *The World Factbook,* 1995.

previous chapter, a number of reforming nonmarket economies —Russia and Vietnam, for example—are following China's lead and attempting to join the WTO. More are likely to follow. Several other countries, such as Saudi Arabia and Taiwan, which are not nonmarket economies but are still not members of the world trading system, are also seeking WTO membership. Individually, each of these countries is significant and their collective GDP exceeds $4.5 trillion (see Table 10.1). This is a relatively small figure compared to the combined GDP of WTO members, but it still reflects a significant trade opportunity.

Given the timing of and international focus on the Chinese application, it is likely to be the first to be resolved. Further, given the strength of China's economy and its trade success, the arrangements struck with China will set a strong precedent for future WTO applications. Certainly, smaller economies can argue powerfully that they should not be held to a higher standard than

China. In effect, with the possible exception of Taiwan, which has accepted developed country status,[29] the China WTO accession agreement could well be a high-water mark for future accession agreements, with many subsequent applicants seeking still more favorable treatment.

Thus, if China were granted effective exemptions from provisions on intellectual property, subsidies, and TRIMs provisions, other applicants would seek the same exemptions. The result would be more freeriders upon the trading system. Since many of the new applicants have stronger economies than some current WTO members, such a situation would be simply unacceptable to many. As discussed in a previous section, given the political environment, even the United States would have difficulty accepting such an unwarranted double standard. The result could be the destruction of the WTO as an effective policeman of international trade and perhaps as an institution.

A weakened WTO could have a serious negative impact on the world economy. The world trading system has been responsible for enormous global growth. Since its creation, the world trading system has brought global average tariffs down from 40 percent to 6.3 percent.[30] Full implementation of the WTO would lower tariffs from the current 6.3 percent to 3.9 percent for developed countries and discipline range of other trade barriers, including subsidies, investment and nontariff barriers. When all provisions are phased in, it is estimated that the WTO could create as much as $500 billion in new global growth by 2005.[31] If the WTO loses credibility and its provisions are not implemented, much of these benefits will be lost. It is also possible that new trade barriers would be raised. In sum, the precedent set by China's WTO application will have far-reaching implications.

**Interim Protections**

The preceding discussion has demonstrated some of the risks of a poorly negotiated WTO accession agreement with China. There are, however, also risks to waiting. As the previous chapter pointed out, China's mercantilism is already taking a toll on global commerce and its industrial plans are advancing. From China's perspective, its exports are at some risk until it becomes a WTO member.

The rest of the world, however, has options for dealing with Chinese trade policy outside of the WTO. As noted previously, a number of bilateral trade agreements have been struck with China. The United States, for example, has major agreements with China on market access, protection of intellectual property, and trade in textiles. Other countries, notably in the EU, have similar arrangements. In some cases, these agreements represent substantial achievements. The intellectual property agreements are actually superior to WTO provisions in patent protection and enforcement. The 1992 market access MOU also has provisions not duplicated in the WTO.

As discussed at some length, there have been substantial compliance problems with these agreements. But there is no reason to think that China will be more inclined to obey the terms of multilateral agreements than bilateral agreements. In whatever forum trade commitments are negotiated, history indicates that enforcement will always be a challenge.

Beyond bilateral diplomacy, unilateral trade laws and other measures can also be used to address trade problems with China. The United States has made extensive use of two of its trade laws in this effort—antidumping laws and Section 301.

U.S. antidumping laws have been used to counter unfairly priced Chinese imports in recent years, with China becoming the leading target of U.S. antidumping actions.[32] The reason for the surge in antidumping actions against China was discussed in Part II. In practical terms, however, antidumping laws do provide at least a temporary solution to some trade problems with China. Antidumping duties provide temporary protection from the effect of Chinese subsidies, state-trading, and export mercantilism within the U.S. market. Although the WTO includes provisions on extending antidumping protection to third markets, these provisions are only in their infancy. Antidumping duties also provide at least a limited incentive for China to undertake economic reforms to eliminate subsidies and other trade barriers.

Section 301 is a provision of U.S. trade law that seeks to enforce trade agreements, eliminate trade barriers, and combat foreign piracy of intellectual property. Section 301 works by identifying foreign trade problems and initiating bilateral negotiations to address them under threat of U.S. trade retaliation if the negotiations fail.[33] Section 301 has been the driving force behind most recent U.S.-China trade diplomacy. Both the 1992 market access MOU and the intellectual property agreements were negotiated under Section 301,[34] and it has been triggered to enforce the intellectual property agreements. Section 301 could also be used to enforce other trade agreements, such as the 1992 market access MOU, if the U.S. administration were so inclined.

In fact, it is worth noting that Section 301 has some advantages over the WTO. As noted, the agreements struck with China on intellectual property and market access using Section 301 are in some ways superior to WTO provisions on the same topics. Section 301 essentially employs the leverage of access to the U.S. market to gain trade concessions from U.S. trading partners; as such, it is a very flexible tool not encumbered by such concerns as developing country status.

If China were a WTO member, Section 301 would actually become a somewhat less effective tool. Section 301 usually works by threatening to raise tariffs on products from the country that is the target of Section 301 negotiations, in this case, China. If China were a WTO member and the United States raised tariffs on Chinese goods without first gaining WTO approval, China could actually protest the U.S. action to the WTO and likely win.[35] In effect, then, if China were a WTO member, Section 301 could still be used to hold China to its WTO commitments, but it probably could not be used to pressure China to make concessions beyond those required by the WTO.

China's other trading partners have similar options. The EU, for example, has also brought numerous antidumping actions against China. After the United States concluded market access and intellectual property agreements with China, the EU struck virtually identical agreements. Further, the EU has simply imposed unilateral quotas on Chinese goods that disrupted or threatened to disrupt the EU market. Despite China's protests, the EU maintains quotas on Chinese products. The number of these quotas has been actually tightened in the last year.[36]

With these interim protections in place, the reader might wonder if there is any reason to move forward with China's WTO membership. The answer to the question is that there is no urgent need; the interim measures can be effective for some time. Ultimately, however, there is a need for a more comprehensive approach to trade problems with China. Actually eliminating Chinese subsidies and mercantilistic state-trading practices through WTO negotiations would eliminate all the negative fallout of these practices instead of just countering some of the impact, as antidumping duties do. The EU's quotas also address symptoms, not the root cause of problems.

Section 301 could theoretically eliminate many Chinese trading practices; however, there are political limits. Section 301 ultimately involves threatening China with unilateral trade sanctions. Given the long list of diplomatic issues between the United States and China on matters as diverse as arms control and sea lanes, it is probably not realistic to expect a U.S. administration to threaten China with a trade war over each of twenty-five to thirty trade issues.

Further, even though China runs a large trade surplus with the United States, it has some market leverage vis-à-vis the United States. The Chinese export market is growing quickly and many U.S. companies are heavily invested in China and in U.S.-China trade; these companies are unlikely to welcome continuing threats of trade sanctions. If the United States carried through on these threats, U.S. companies in China would likely be targets of Chinese counterretaliation. Thus, the interests of U.S. companies could pose a barrier to wider use of Section 301. Already, during the recent round of trade retaliation threats surrounding protection of intellectual property, some U.S. companies expressed reservations over sanction threats.[37]

A single, broad negotiation to address many of these issues in the WTO context is, thus, attractive in the long run. This is not to say that the WTO would automatically solve all problems. Vigorous monitoring and ongoing discussions are certain to be necessary. If the experience with bilateral agreements is any guide, a few heated trade conflicts are likely to flare. Still, WTO accession negotiations do offer a significant opportunity to make progress on a range of important trade and economic issues with China, progress that would be difficult, if not impossible, to match through other means.

China's interests in joining the WTO are also continuing but are probably not urgent. With its growing economic strength and diplomatic influence, China can bring significant resources to bear in a trade conflict and, given the importance of export markets to China, it would likely do just that if its exports were threatened.

This is not a permanent solution for China, however, for it fails to fulfill China's ambition to gain the status and recognition associated with being a member of the world trading system. Further, there are still threats to China's exports great and small. Most threatening to China are small trade problems, like the EU quotas and antidumping actions, which have a negative impact upon trade, but not so significant that China can easily escalate the matter. It is not clear how much WTO membership would help, at least with antidumping actions, but China does seem to think it would be helpful in addressing these issues. It is also possible that another crisis, like Tiananmen Square, could trigger broad trade sanctions against China. A country as dependent on exports as China must be concerned over both of these threats and would likely welcome the additional protection that WTO membership can provide.

## Conclusion

The previous chapter concluded by citing the enormous potential opportunity that China's accession to the WTO creates. This chapter should appropriately add to that valid conclusion that this enormous opportunity will require effort to exploit and carries with it some major risks.

Consider the following hypothetical scenario. Tensions between the western world and China remain high over a series of arms control and territorial issues. In order to decrease tensions, the United States decides to sacrifice economic interests to gain goodwill from China, as it has done with numerous countries during the Cold War. The United States, which has led most of the negotiations with China, and other WTO members accept China's contention that it should be allowed to join the WTO as a developing country. In doing so, China is granted an effective pass on many WTO provisions and is able to continue pursuing its mercantilistic trade and industrial policies.

After a very few years, these Chinese policies bear fruit. China is able to run up enormous trade surpluses with the world. The mercantilistic strategy also succeeds in severely harming otherwise competitive western industries. China becomes a new Japan.

Seeing China's success, and seeing that the WTO is not effective in curbing mercantilism, many countries in Asia, Eastern Europe, and perhaps even Russia follow suit. Within a few more years, there is a growing number of copycat economies following the Japan/China path to economic success through mercantilism. Since these countries all entered the WTO on the same flexible terms as China, the WTO is of no help in disciplining their strategies. The WTO does, however, keep the United States and other western countries from using the threat of trade sanctions to curb this wave of mercantilism.

As trade deficits rise and industries lay off workers, support for free trade in the developed world, including the United States, fails. In order to protect their economies from the new mercantilists, countries in the developed world raise trade barriers. Free trade and the world trading system suffer a major setback and global growth is stunted.

It goes without saying that this is a worst-case scenario but not an entirely unrealistic one. All of the links in the chain of events that it envisages are possible and even likely outcomes of the failure to adequately address the issues raised by China entering the WTO.

The lesson is simple: The prospect of China's joining the WTO is a double-edged sword. On the one hand, the potential benefits of a smoothly handled integration are enormous. On the other hand, if key issues are bungled, the downside risks are equally enormous. This is not to say that the integration of China into the world economy and the trading system should not go forward. Given political and economic trends, such an integration now appears inevitable. It is only to say that caution is dictated.

## Notes

1. Nicholas R. Lardy, *China in the World Economy* (Washington, DC: Institute for International Economics, April 1994), 141–43.

2. Greg Mastel, *China and the WTO: Economy at the Crossroad* (Washington, DC: Economic Strategy Institute, 1994).

3. Ambassador Charlene Barshefsky, *Testimony Before the Senate Finance Committee,* June 6, 1996.

4. "Commission Proposed New Policy on China," *Reuter European Community Report,* July 5, 1995.

5. It is perhaps more accurate to call the WTO the second major institution to integrate China, since it was recently admitted to the International Monetary Fund. The implications of China's joining the WTO are, however, far more sweeping.

6. P.T. Bangsberg, "Chinese Aim to Facilitate GATT Re-Entry," *Journal of Commerce,* March 8, 1993.

7. World Bank, *World Debt Tables, External Financing for Developing Countries* (Washington, DC: The World Bank, March 12, 1996), 29.

8. John Jackson, *The World Trading System: Law and Policy of International Economic Relations* (Cambridge, MA: The MIT Press, 1994), 278.

9. Ibid., 20.

10. World Bank, *India; Economic Development* (Washington, DC: The World Bank, 1996).

11. Danny M. Leipziger and Vinod Thomas, *An Overview of Country Experience* (Washington, DC: The World Bank, 1993); Teck-Wong Soon and C. Suan Tan, *Singapore: Public Policy and Economic Development* (Washington, DC: The World Bank, 1993).

12. Laura D'Andrea Tyson, *Who's Bashing Whom? Trade Conflict in High Technology Industries* (Washington, DC: Institute for International Economics, 1992).

13. Chalmers Johnson, *Japan: Who Governs?* (New York: W.W. Norton,

1995); and Kihwan Kim and Danny M. Leipziger, *The Lessons of East Asia. Korea: A Case of Government-Led Development* (Washington, DC: World Bank, 1993).

14. Ibid., and Danny M. Leipziger and Peter Petri, *Korean Industrial Policy: Legacy of the Past and Directions for the Future* (Washington, DC: The World Bank, 1993).

15. United States Trade Representative, *Uruguay Round of Multilateral Trade Negotiations General Agreements on Tariffs and Trade* (Washington, DC: U.S. Government Printing Office, 1994), 385–86.

16. Refer to Table 2.7 on page 25.

17. Ministry of Foreign Economic Relations and Trade, *Almanac of China's Foreign Economic Relations and Trade, 1993,* 479; U.S. Department of Commerce trade statistics.

18. See, for examples, *Final Act Embodying the Results of the Uruguay Round of Multilateral Trade Negotiations,* Decisions on Measures in Favor of Least Developed Countries, April 15, 1994.

19. *Final Act,* Agreement on Trade Related Aspects of Intellectual Property Rights, Articles 65 and 66.

20. *Final Act,* Agreement on Government Procurement, Article V.

21. *Final Act,* Agreement on Subsidies and Countervailing Measures, Part VIII.

22. *Final Act,* Agreement on Trade Related Investment Measures, Article 4.

23. *Final Act,* Agreement on Subsidies and Countervailing Measures, Part VIII, Articles 27.2 through 27.5.

24. Ibid., Annex VII.

25. Ibid., Article 29.1.

26. *Final Act,* Agreement on Trade Related Investment Measures, Article 4.

27. *Memorandum of Understanding Between the Government of the People's Republic of China and the Government of the United States of America on the Protection of Intellectual Property,* 1992, and *Memorandum of Understanding Between the Government of the People's Republic of China and the Government of the United States of America on the Protection of Intellectual Property,* 1995.

28. Ambassador Charlene Barshefsky, *Testimony Before the House Ways and Means Committee,* September 19, 1996, document not yet published.

29. Ibid.; and Christian Murck, *Testimony Before the House Ways and Means Committee,* September 19, 1996, document not yet published.

30. *Economic Report of the President, 1992* (Washington, DC: U.S. Government Printing Office, 1992), 210.

31. Joseph F. François, Bradley McDonald, and Keikan Nordstrom, *The Uruguay Round: A Global General Equilibrium Assessment* (Geneva: GATT Secretariat, 1993).

32. U.S. International Trade Commission, *Annual Reports 1993–1995* (Washington, DC: U.S. ITC, 1993–1995).

33. Greg Mastel, *American Trade Laws after the Uruguay Round* (Armonk, NY: M.E. Sharpe, 1996), Sec.1.

34. Ibid., 22.

35. Ibid., 142.

36. "Commission Deems It Has 'Evident Proof' of Fraud Concerning Origins and Reduces Certain Import Quotas for Textiles," *Reuter European Community Report,* January 25, 1996.

37. Jack Robertson, "U.S. Firms Unfazed by Sanction Threat," *Electronic Buyers' News,* June 17, 1996.

# 11

# A Strategy for Integration

As Part II outlined, there are numerous barriers to integrating China into the WTO. In addition to traditional trade barriers, there are problems with China's lack of a rule of law, its totalitarian government, and its governmental distortions of foreign exchange markets. The task is not insurmountable, but it is difficult and will take time. It is simply not realistic to expect China to establish a rule of law, reform its government, create a new foreign exchange regime, or even phase out all WTO-inconsistent trade barriers overnight. The transition will take time.

That raises the topic of this chapter, the strategy and mechanics for making a transition from China's current trade and foreign exchange regime to one compatible with the WTO. A successful transition scheme must meet three general criteria. First, it must take place over a finite, relatively short period of time. An endless special status without an endpoint would be essentially the same as developing country status and would undermine the credibility of the WTO. China should be given adequate time to make the transition, but that period should be short, substantially shorter than the century China has requested. China cannot be allowed to become a freerider on the trading system.

Second, China must be bound to undertake concrete legal and economic reforms. At the end of the transition period, China's trade and foreign exchange regime should be fully in compliance with the WTO. The rule of law should be functioning, at least in the commercial area, and governmental powers should be restricted to the point that they do not interfere with normal commerce.

Finally, the agreement must be enforceable and must ensure that the expected trade benefits are forthcoming. Chinese officials may express concern over the unique focus on enforcement, but China's poor record in implementing trade agreements and general lack of rule of law make such attention essential. The transition must be real and must result in new export opportunities for China's trading partners. Dismantling one set of barriers only to have them replaced with another set is simply not sufficient.

If an adequate transition to WTO membership were made, the door would be open to continue integrating China into the world economy with eventual membership in other institutions.

As hard as this path to reform will be for China, it imposes nearly equal challenges upon China's trading partners. For major trading countries, there is the task of retaining relative unanimity to ensure that China receives a consistent message on the need to reform. Currently, China has shown itself adept at playing the United States, the EU, and Japan off each other in the hope of getting one or the other to support its goal of a painless, reform-free path to WTO membership. Surprisingly, China has had some success.[1]

In addition, each of the major trading powers has had difficulty maintaining a consistent message to China. Different cabinet agencies appear to have different views as to the timing and requirements of WTO membership for China and their statements reflect these differences.[2] The EU produced a very strong paper on China's WTO membership in the fall of 1995, but statements of political leaders have seemed to back away from that position paper.[3] In the summer of 1996, Prime Minister Hashimoto of Japan advocated quick membership in the WTO for China.[4] A few days later, Japan seemed to qualify the statement by stating that it meant membership only after reform.

The central challenge facing the key trading powers—the United States, the EU, and Japan—is simply to keep a consistent message both internally and externally. Of course, small differences on priorities are inevitable and acceptable, but all must keep focus on the central demand that China make economic and legal reforms in return for WTO membership. If they cannot maintain consistency, China will likely simply wait with the expectation that the conflict will eventually lead to its gaining membership without reform.

Those, then, are some of the considerable economic and diplomatic challenges that must be addressed by a strategy to integrate China into the WTO.

## A Transition

Initially, U.S. trade negotiators were unwilling to concede to their Chinese counterparts that a transition period was necessary for China to enter the WTO.[5] Against the backdrop of this discussion, their position may not seem entirely reasonable. Of course, China's request for a century-long phase-in is also not, to say the least, entirely reasonable either. U.S. negotiators probably took this position not because they believed no transition would be necessary, but because they wanted the discussion to focus on substantive reform, not transition periods and special treatment.

As sound as this bargaining strategy is, however, a transition period is necessary. The reforms that China must undertake simply cannot be accomplished immediately. There are both political and economic limits upon reform. Just the task of phasing out impermissible subsidization to SOEs will, at least temporarily, unemploy a number of Chinese workers. Since it is still ostensibly a command economy, China does not yet have a comprehensive system for managing unemployment. The disparities between the coastal provinces and the interior provinces have led to the development of a large transient work force made up of millions working and living without government documentation. This leads to serious economic and social problems for China. Further, the heated debate over economic reform that sometimes appears in the Chinese press and in other political forums indicates that there are also political limits upon economic reform in China.[6]

Of course, the best remedy for most of these economic and

social problems is continued economic growth, which is best spurred by increasing the pace of economic reform. Unfortunately, this strong economic logic does not eliminate the real adjustment costs that China faces. Experience from around the world indicates that countries need time to adjust to such challenges.

This should not, however, be taken as an excuse to effectively halt reform with endless transition periods. Further, China should not enjoy the full benefits of WTO membership until it also shoulders the responsibilities of membership. Withholding the full benefits of membership until China has completed economic reforms is, ultimately, the only leverage to ensure that the transition takes place.

### Nonmarket Economies and the World Trading System

The central question is not, "Will there be a transition period?" All observers concede that China is incapable of immediately adopting all the reforms necessary to come into compliance with the WTO. The real questions are "How long will the transition be?" and "What will be China's interim status and responsibilities?" Fortunately, there is some historical precedent for addressing those questions.

In the 1950s and early 1960s, several Eastern European countries took advantage of flexibility from Moscow to begin experimenting with market economics. As part of these experiments, three Eastern European countries—Poland, Romania, and Hungary—sought membership in the world trading system on the theory that increased trade with the West would bolster their economies.[7]

At the time there was significant debate over whether to accept these applications for GATT membership. Many European voices argued that, as nonmarket economies, these three candidates were simply ill equipped for membership in the market trading system. Given their proximity, European officials also expressed concern that their markets might be disrupted by dumped and subsidized products from the Eastern European applicants. Canada and Japan expressed similar concerns about market disruptions, inadequate export opportunities, and the general difficulties with integrating nonmarket economies into the market trading system.[8]

The United States, however, took a different view. Apparently seeing these applications as an opportunity to lure away some of the Soviet Union's satellite states, and probably seeing little real threat of trade problems with such small economies, the United States pressed strongly for acceptance of the applications.[9]

The United States eventually prevailed, but serious concerns were expressed. As the GATT executive secretary noted in 1960:

> Whilst [interest in accession by centrally planned economies] has been welcomed in principle by the Contracting Parties, serious questions have been raised as to whether the GATT rules as they stand could provide the basis for real balance in trading opportunities and advantages between a contracting party with a centrally planned economy. . . . It may well be time for resuming the attempt that was made during the GATT trade discussions to spell out trading rules to fit the situation. . . . There may be other ways of dealing with it, but it is emerging as a problem which cannot be indefinitely ignored.[10]

The solution ultimately settled upon to "spell out trading rules to fit the situation" consisted of unique accession agreements with the nonmarket economies aimed at smoothing the transition and addressing the special concerns raised by their nonmarket status. Each of the three agreements had some differences tailored to the unique economic structure of each nonmarket economy. In Hungary's case, much weight was given, probably inappropriately, to an economic reform package that Hungary was contemplating. As a result, the accession agreement with Hungary was not too different from those struck with other market-oriented applicants. The agreements with Poland and Romania, however, contained some truly innovative and notable provisions.[11]

First, given the planned nature of the economies, there was concern that export opportunities would not emerge in these countries. The fear was that the countries might stifle exports through government controls or prefer to import from other

Eastern European nations or the Soviet Union instead of GATT members. The solution to this problem was the most innovative feature of the agreements: import growth targets. Poland was obligated to increase imports from GATT members by 7 percent per year. Romania was obligated to ensure that imports from GATT members grew at least as quickly as imports from communist bloc countries.[12]

Second, these countries lacked a currency that was easily convertible to western currencies, and their governments maintained extensive controls over foreign exchange. GATT members feared that this could result in currency values being manipulated to gain trade advantages and other interferences with foreign exchange. The solution involved some innovative commitments to ensure convertibility and to bar manipulation of foreign exchange.[13]

Third, in response to the concerns of Europe and other GATT members that their markets would be deluged by subsidized Eastern European products, a special safeguard provision was included in the agreements. In the language of the international trading system, safeguards are temporary import barriers put in place to avoid serious market disruptions. All trading system members can impose safeguards on the exports of other system members, but the standard for imposing the safeguards is high and the safeguards are tightly regulated as to coverage and duration. The safeguards on the nonmarket economies' exports had a lower threshold for action and fewer regulations. In essence, the result of these safeguards was that Europe and other GATT members were able to impose temporary import limits upon the exports of Poland, Romania, and Hungary if those exports disrupted or threatened to disrupt their markets.[14] In Europe's case, these safeguards would have been practically identical to the import quotas Europe today imposes on Chinese exports that disrupt European markets.

The final provision of note was the so-called general safeguard provision. The general safeguard was established in the accession protocols.[15] Basically, the general safeguard was a trade emergency brake that GATT members could trigger if serious problems arose. The effect would have been to terminate the accession agreement and put trade back on the basis that it existed before the accession arrangement was put in place. The general safeguard could also work as an enforcement mechanism, with GATT members triggering it if they felt the nonmarket economy was not upholding its commitments.

In the mid-1970s, the Soviet Union reasserted economic control over its satellites, economic conditions changed, GATT members lost interest in the accession process, and these accession agreements largely ceased to be relevant. In the interim, however, they succeeded. In terms of new export opportunities, the rather nonspecific Romanian targets are difficult to evaluate, but Romanian imports did increase.[16] As a result of the combination of the 7 percent import target, foreign exchange commitments, other provisions of the accession protocol, and other factors, Poland's imports between 1968 and 1976 increased an average of 27.3 percent per year; Polish imports rose 18 percent in 1971, 48.9 percent in 1972, 65.3 percent in 1973, 41.8 percent in 1974, 15.1 percent in 1975, and 11.4 percent in 1976 (the average was calculated on a compounded basis). Poland's imports increased by more than 7 percent in all but one year.[17]

Of course, it is impossible to determine how much the provisions of the accession agreement contributed to the dramatic increase in Poland's imports from GATT members. Other economic factors could certainly have had an impact, and it is difficult twenty-five years after the fact to make a comprehensive study. Still, it certainly seems more than coincidental that the dramatic increases occurred during the period of the accession agreement. The import targets and other provisions seem to have succeeded in creating new export opportunities for GATT members in these Eastern European countries.

During this period, the exports of Poland and Romania to GATT members also rose. From 1969 to 1974, Poland's exports to GATT members also grew more quickly than exports to other countries. Somewhat surprisingly, however, there were no reports of special safeguards being triggered as of 1975. As one history of the protocols notes, "no case of market disruption of [Polish] exports with the effects of subsidization was notified, nor had any concrete proof been offered with regard to possible direct or indirect subsidy effects of Polish exports."[18] Again, the causes are difficult to determine. It may simply be that Poland's industries were not competitive enough or its economy not large enough to cause real problems. On the whole, these three nonmarket economy accession agreements were generally successful. The provisions of the agreements, including safeguards and import targets, could prove quite useful in handling the same trade problems with China three and a half decades later.

Chinese officials bristle somewhat at the suggestion that these models could be applied to present day China, although, when convenient, they also cite them as examples to support their positions. The argument they make is that the three economies were generally less market oriented than China is today and had less sophisticated trading regimes.

This argument is true as far as it goes but is not a particularly compelling argument against applying this precedent to China. Certainly, China is a larger and more competitive economy, but it is still a largely centrally planned economy. In some cases, the increased strength of the Chinese economy as compared to that of the three earlier nonmarket economies could make the application of a special safeguard more important. Chinese exports certainly have more potential to disrupt markets. As already noted, the EU currently has safeguard-like quotas on Chinese exports. If such a provision existed for China, it is not likely to go unused, as it did in Poland's case.

It is true that China has a more sophisticated foreign trade regime than the three nonmarket economies that joined the GATT. It is also true that one of the reasons that the 7 percent target was chosen for Poland was that Poland did not have a traditional trade regime relying upon tariffs and such; it relied instead on central planning.[19] China has tariffs and quotas, but, as the previous section made clear, it also has an operating central economic plan that restricts trade. Just as the concern with Poland was that, absent some provision, the central planning machinery could block and distort trade, China's central planning machinery has enormous potential to distort trade—even if all tariffs and traditional barriers are eliminated. Thus, in China's case, it would be appropriate to engage in a traditional accession negotiation aimed at lowering tariffs, eliminating quotas, and so forth. However, it would also be appropriate to employ import targets to ensure that the machinery of central planning is not allowed to render all of the traditional trade concessions moot.

China is certainly different than Poland, Romania, and Hungary, but the differences do not invalidate the innovative accession protocols used in those earlier cases. In fact, since China is a larger and more competitive centrally planned economy, many of the provisions in those protocols are even more important in China's case.

## The U.S. Position

Historically, the United States has enjoyed a "first among equals" status in the world trading system. According to U.S. statistics, the United States is China's largest trading partner. Since relations with China have many geopolitical dimensions, the United States, as the Cold War leader of the free world, played a role in defining the direction of China's relationship with the West.

These factors are less influential now than they were even a few years ago. With the collapse of the Soviet Union, U.S. allies feel more free than ever to set their own foreign policy independent of U.S. positions. Given its geographic proximity and the long history involved, Japan in particular looks at China independently of the United States. Attracted to the potential of China's market, many countries seem even less likely to look to the United States for leadership on China policy in the future.

Nonetheless, up to the present, the United States has been the de facto leader of GATT/WTO negotiations on Chinese accession. Of course, the working party, with a Swiss chairman, is independent of the United States, although the United States is a member. But the United States has taken the lead in defining the issues for the negotiations and winning support for its position among other trading countries. Further, the overall tenor of U.S.-China relations has had a direct impact on the atmosphere and general prospects for the accession process.

The United States has also developed more detailed positions on China's accession than other countries. Thus, an analysis of the current state of the negotiations appropriately begins by analyzing U.S. positions. This task is more difficult than it may seem because U.S. negotiators have made considerable efforts to keep a large portion of their position papers out of the public eye. The most significant document relevant to this discussion is the so-called "road map" that the United States presented to China in November 1995.[20] As of this writing, however, the document has not been formally made public.

Based upon press reports and discussions with negotiators, the road map is simply an outline of the key steps that China must take in order to secure WTO membership. Without specifically referencing negotiating documents, eight aspects of the U.S. position are worthy of note.

First, the United States seems willing to accept a phase-in period for China's WTO responsibilities, although few details of the nature and length of this transition have been settled. The United States has made clear, however, that a never-defined transitional concept known as the "halfway house," advanced by EU trade minister Leon Brittan, is not acceptable. Apparently, the halfway house concept extends to China a lower-tier membership to the WTO. The details of this tiered membership concept were never released, but both U.S. and Chinese negotiators expressed concern, and it appears not to be allowable under WTO rules.[21]

Second, U.S. negotiators have made it clear on several occasions that the issue of WTO membership for China, though not formally linked to other issues, is not to be considered in a vacuum. At different times, senior U.S. officials have linked WTO membership to enforcement of the intellectual property agreement and U.S.-Chinese relations more generally.[22]

Third, and not at all surprisingly, the United States and all other countries involved in WTO talks with China have emphasized increased access to the Chinese market. The United States, in particular, has drafted papers on trading rights, tariffs, import licenses, and a range of other market access issues. Other countries have also raised concerns of particular relevance to their potential export opportunities. For example, Australia, a leading grain exporter, has been interested in the prospects for increasing grain exports to China. Market access concerns typically are at the core of accession negotiations and this negotiation appears to be no exception.

Fourth, the United States has worked to define a special safeguard procedure applicable to China. Given its history, the EU has also taken an interest in special safeguards.[23] Formally, Chinese negotiators have opposed any safeguard that would be applied only to China. Informally, however, Chinese negotiators seem to recognize that some such provision will be part of a final agreement.

Thus far, the main issue regarding special safeguards has been the test to be applied before a safeguard could be triggered. Since safeguards are applied as a temporary measure to allow adjustment to exports against which there is no allegation of unfair trading, the standard applied before they can be imposed is rigorous. A country wishing to impose a safeguard must demonstrate serious economic injury from imports and apply the safeguard only to the imports responsible for the injury. In China's case, the EU has proposed a much lower market disruption test. Defining the specifics of the test to be applied and the length of time the special safeguard will operate seem destined to be the key points needing resolution on this issue.

Fifth, the United States has proposed a general safeguard provision, like that included in the Romania, Poland, and Hungary accession agreements. Initially, this was interpreted as a way in which the United States could allow China to join the WTO without amending the Jackson–Vanik legislation, which prevented the United States from granting the cornerstone of WTO membership, unconditional MFN status, to any communist country. Though it may be possible to use a general safeguard in this manner, U.S. negotiators have stated that this is not their intention. Instead, the U.S. negotiators apparently view the general safeguard just as it was conceived in previous accession agreements, as a general circuit breaker and potential enforcement mechanism.

Sixth, the United States and the EU have expressed concern over Chinese investment performance requirements. The United States has focused on technology transfer requirements. The EU, for its part, has been more concerned over the export and trade balancing requirements.

Seventh, the United States has indicated that the Jackson–Vanik Amendment will force it to take a nonapplication exception to China. Ironically, this would mean that after all the time and effort taken to negotiate a WTO accession agreement, it would not directly effect U.S.-China trade relations. The United States and China would still be forced by the U.S. Jackson–Vanik law to conduct their trade relations outside of the WTO. Of course, it would probably be possible to negotiate a bilateral agreement to mirror the provisions of the WTO agreement. It might even be possible to use WTO panels to mediate U.S.-China disputes, if both sides were willing. Formally though, the trading relationship would remain outside the WTO.[24]

This situation is obviously awkward. It also creates the potential of the United States being excluded from final negotiations on China's WTO accessions, thus lessening U.S. bargaining leverage vis-à-vis China. This fact, coupled with growing dissatisfaction with Jackson–Vanik's requirement for an annual congressional vote on MFN for China, has spurred a number of calls for reform or for elimination of Jackson–Vanik. The author, for example, has suggested offering to eliminate Jackson–Vanik in return for trade concessions from China.[25] The outcome of this domestic U.S. debate is unclear, however, and there is significant support in Congress for reviewing Chinese behavior on human rights and other issues annually under Jackson–Vanik.

Eighth and finally, the United States has somewhat tentatively raised the issue of using import targets as a transitional measure with China. The United States has pointed out that such measures were employed not only with Poland and Romania but also in other recent WTO agreements.[26]

Although it could always be affected by domestic political concerns or U.S.-China relations in general, the United States does appear prepared, after a recent round of high-level diplomacy, to move forward on China's WTO accession with the aim of conclusion in the near term.

**Multilateral Diplomacy**

For reasons just outlined, however, the views of the United States on China's accession are not as important as they once were. Other countries seem inclined to look at this issue with less concern for the U.S. perspective. As a member of the working group on China's application, the United States could block formation of the consensus necessary to advance China's application to a final vote. Yet such a unilateral strategy would likely expose the United States to both diplomatic criticism and potential retaliation from China, so the United States is unlikely to block China's application alone.

Thus, the views of other countries on China's accession are quite important. Two other players have had a significant role and could be even more important as talks advance: the EU and Japan. The EU has been active in these talks for several years, with EU representatives negotiating with the Chinese on market access and other issues of interest to Europe. As noted in the previous discussion, U.S. and EU positions on key issues have been generally consistent. In 1995, the EU commission produced a "white paper," which, though it differed from the U.S. position on a few points, took very much the same position on key issues as the United States. Both EU and U.S. negotiators characterized their working relationship in these negotiations as good.[27]

Not all developments point to future unity, however. A number of member states of the EU, notably France and Germany, have taken pains to build a positive relationship with China attracted by business opportunities there.[28] National leaders have also made more positive comments on China's WTO candidacy after meeting with Chinese leaders. EU trade minister Leon Brittan has taken a seemingly erratic position on this issue. Though formal EU positions have been supportive of U.S. positions, Brittan's statements have called on China and the United States to compromise. His statements consistently paint the EU as more supportive of China's membership in the WTO than the United States.[29]

Concerned about criticism of its own trade surplus and trade practices, Japan has historically not played an active role in the trading system, preferring to stay in the background and react to other countries' initiatives. It has, however, grown more assertive in the WTO and seems to be positioning itself to take a more active role on China's WTO accession. Along with a number of other countries, Japan is a member of the working group on China's WTO accession and has held bilateral consultations with China. Recently, Japan has taken an even more activist stance by announcing in July 1996 that it favored immediate WTO membership for China and intended to hold educational sessions on this issue for other economic powers through G-7 meetings.[30] It is difficult to interpret these Japanese moves, especially since further Japanese statements have indicated that Japan favors membership for China only after it has undertaken economic and trade reforms; if this is the case, Japan's position is not much different from that of the United States and the EU.

As this brief discussion of recent developments should make clear, the WTO negotiations with China promise to become complicated diplomatically as well as substantively. The combination of declining U.S. influence and increasing Chinese leverage has made the diplomacy behind these talks unusually complicated. At times, there have been indications of splits and disagreements within the governments of each of the major WTO members engaged in these talks. In addition, both the EU and Japan seem inclined to paint the United States as the "heavy" to curry favor with China; this was particularly apparent during recent U.S. efforts to enforce an intellectual property agreement with China.

Despite these efforts at diplomatic one-upmanship, however, the United States, Europe, Japan, and all of the countries in the trading system share similar interests. All stand to have their trade and economic interests harmed by Chinese mercantilism. Realistically, the potential damage that Chinese mercantilism could do to each of their economies far outweighs whatever transient benefits that might be gained from China, such as aircraft sales or subway construction contracts. Unfortunately, negotiations are being conducted in an atmosphere of new post–Cold War diplomacy; countries do not have much experience with the new situation and the rules have not yet been defined. Against this backdrop, keeping focused on long-term interests will be a challenge for all of the countries involved.

If this challenge is not met, however, China is likely to simply wait and hope that the conflict and confusion allow it to gain WTO membership without undertaking further reform. As the previous discussion should make clear, if China is successful in this effort, all countries and the world economy will end up losing. Hopefully, that threat will be enough to keep diplomatic jockeying from obscuring long-term interests.

### A Plan for China's WTO Membership

In light of the substantive problems and political complications just noted, the question can once again be asked, Is it possible to integrate China into the world economy? The answer remains, however, that integration is an inevitable reality that advances each day with every Chinese export and every new investment in China. The key question is how it can best be managed. In the short term, the WTO is likely the most useful tool for integration, but this will not be a simple matter. In the last several decades, major new countries, such as Japan and Mexico,[31] have joined the world trading system, but those countries did not pose as serious a challenge as does integrating China into the WTO. The challenge is large, but it is surmountable if a strategy based on the following five elements is pursued.

First and foremost, to be deemed successful, a WTO agreement must obligate China to observe all WTO disciplines within a fixed period of time. In the past, as in the case of Japan, trading system rules have been bent to allow early admission of a country into the trading system. The ill effects resulting from Japan's early entry are well known.[32] Less well known are the enormous economic distortions that have been allowed to continue and even been accentuated by the ill-considered decision to allow developing countries to ignore trading rules. The end result of the inclusion of developing country status in the GATT has been a two-tiered system: members and freeriders. If the list of freeriders grows longer, the system will be increasingly unable to bear the economic and political strain they create. Ironically, freerider status often seems to have actually retarded economic development instead of speeding it. Developing country status is truly a lose–lose proposition.[33]

Allowing China to join the rolls of the freeriders risks turning a nagging problem into a crisis. All the potential economic benefits of further economic reform in China would be lost. The precedent set could well destroy the entire trading system as developed countries tire of carrying the burden of global growth. The world economy simply cannot allow China to become an enormous freerider on the trading system.

In practical terms, this means that China must halt the creation of new trade barriers and mercantilistic industrial plans. Such a measure is often called a standstill agreement. It should stop China from simply replacing one trade barrier with another.

Further, China must be obligated to bring its trading regime fully into WTO compliance in a fixed period of, at most, a decade. This means dismantling all WTO-inconsistent trade barriers, including subsidies and trade-distorting investment practices, and establishing a rule of law, which includes a reliable domestic judicial process. The Chinese government must also establish a record of fulfilling trade commitments. Probably most difficult for China, WTO compliance also means allowing the market to function without the interference of the machinery of communism. Some of the most onerous aspects of the system, such as government control of trading rights, should be abolished immediately.

Second, an accession protocol should establish both specific and general safeguard provisions. Since China is likely to be allowed to continue operating subsidy programs and other trade-distorting policies for a period of some years, other WTO members should be allowed to implement special safeguard measures during this phase-in period. The enormous surge in dumping cases involving Chinese products demonstrates the potential magnitude of the problem. Since safeguard actions will often operate to blunt the impact of Chinese trade distortions, the test for triggering a safeguard should be quite liberal. The EU's proposal for a "market disruption" test seems credible. Certainly, the serious injury standard generally employed in safeguard cases is far too high.

An effective general safeguard is also necessary. The negotiators of the accession protocols with Poland and other Eastern European countries recognized the enormous complexity of integrating a nonmarket economy into the trading system and thought a generic circuit breaker or safety provision was wise. Thirty-five years later, the trading system is more complex and imposes more discipline on national economies. Furthermore, China is far bigger than the three small nonmarket economies. A general circuit breaker or safety valve is even more sensible.

A general safeguard could also become the primary enforcement mechanism for the protocol. As noted in Part II, many of the trade problems in China are simply too difficult to document and too widespread to be effectively controlled by a normal WTO dispute settlement process. Particularly during a transition period, in extreme cases, if another member feels China is not abiding by commitments, it should be allowed to withdraw benefits from China without going through time-consuming and ultimately ineffectual dispute settlement procedures. The weaknesses in dispute settlement procedures cannot be allowed to operate as a shield for sub rosa protectionism. Certainly, given the risk of Chinese retaliation, members are not likely to trip this emergency break lightly, but it is a necessary fail-safe for this complicated process.

Third, as was the case with the three nonmarket economies in the 1960s, attention must be paid to foreign exchange issues. At a minimum, China should be required to eliminate all foreign exchange balancing requirements and establish full convertibility for the yuan. It would also be wise to set up a special body, perhaps jointly through the WTO and the IMF, to monitor and advise China on necessary steps to foreign exchange reform. This body could also advise other member countries of potential problems. China should find little to be objectionable about these reforms since it has committed to them in principle.

Fourth, again borrowing from the earlier protocols with Poland and Romania, China should be obligated to increase imports from other WTO members by a fixed percentage each year. This should ensure that the market opportunities reasonably expected to come about as a result of these reforms actually materialize and are not thwarted by Chinese policies. In other words, this provides another enforcement check.

Some may react negatively to the concept of import targets. The idea was employed in attempts to open the Japanese market in the U.S.-Japan Semiconductor Trade Agreement. Because of concern that Japan or Japanese companies might subtly collude to frustrate attempts to open the Japanese semiconductor market, at the United States' urging, negotiators included a 20 percent foreign market share target in the agreement. Substantively, the market opening provision of the Semiconductor Agreement was an enormous success, and the foreign share of the Japanese market rose from 8.5 percent in 1985 to over 30 percent in 1996. Industry observers credit the target as an important factor in making the agreement a success.[34]

Success is not always enough, however, to satisfy critics. Based upon the semiconductor agreement, two criticisms have been leveled at the concept of market share targets to integrate

China into the WTO. The first is that it might be used to discriminate in favor of the exports of certain countries and against those of other countries. The second is that it might distort trade in China and encourage the continued operation of government planning agencies.[35]

The first criticism is the easiest to answer. Even though it was clearly written in terms of foreign market share and not U.S. market share, it was perhaps reasonable to argue that since the United States negotiated the semiconductor agreement, Japanese authorities might seek out U.S. semiconductors and shun those of other countries. This criticism could, of course, not be applied to a multilaterally negotiated WTO accession agreement. If it was a serious concern, it could certainly be monitored by the working group charged with evaluating implementation of China's accession arrangements.

Based on their comments, it sometimes seems that critics are unaware that market share targets are not a new idea to be applied only to China. Actually, they are a market-opening device that has been employed in GATT/WTO negotiations on several occasions. The market share targets included in accession protocols with Poland and Romania have already been discussed at length, but, more recently, market share targets were also an important part of the agricultural section of the Uruguay Round, the agreement that created the WTO. Agriculture was one of the most contentious portions of the Uruguay Round, and one of the most difficult issues was ensuring that agricultural markets were truly opened. In many countries, agricultural trade barriers were high and there was fear of governments finding new, more subtle ways to exclude imports. Therefore, a minimum market share target for agricultural imports in previously protected sectors was inserted into the Uruguay Round agreement.[36] As in this case, market share targets have been used in the multilateral trading system to ensure that markets were truly opened; opening the Chinese market seems to present just the type of challenge that import targets have proven effective in addressing.

The second criticism is more substantive. Obviously, it would be counterproductive to strengthen the Chinese machinery of government interference with the free market. There are, however, two reasons this concern should not be considered serious. First, the agreement would presumably explicitly mandate that this interference end at a certain time. The market share target would operate only in the interim. Second, as noted in the examples above, market share targets have been effective in breaking imports into markets that were previously tightly closed. With an import target, the machinery of central planning can be drafted to work for the market and create opportunities for imports instead of finding ways to exclude them. Further, once imports become familiar to and even preferred by Chinese customers, the targets will have built a constituency for market opening and imports; nothing could be more useful in the task of opening the Chinese market.

The fifth and final element of a transitional arrangement is an ongoing monitoring body. Given the enormity of the task involved, China's accession will require continued monitoring. Unforeseen problems are certain to arise and require attention. Again, as was the case with Poland, Romania, and Hungary, an ongoing working group must be established. On paper, this probably seems the least interesting and least imaginative element of a possible plan for China's entry into the WTO. In reality, however, it is certain to be one of the most important and will likely require as much attention as the accession negotiations.

**Other Institutions**

Because it is the logical and probably necessary first step, this discussion has focused upon the issues associated with integrating China into the WTO. In time, however, China may also be integrated into other institutions, such as the G-7 and the OECD.

At the present time, China is less ready for membership in these institutions than in the WTO. Take the G-7, for example—a body of the world's largest democratic, market economies banded together to manage the world economy. Since China is currently neither a market economy nor a democracy, it seems utterly unprepared for membership. In theory, there are good reasons to consider China for G-7 membership. China would provide some geographic balance to the Eurocentric group. Until it establishes some basic market mechanisms, however, such as an open and fully convertible foreign exchange system, China does not even have the capacity to cooperate in global economic planning.

WTO membership would help to establish many of these mechanisms and complete the process of market reform in China. Thus, a decade after the WTO accession package suggested here is implemented, China might be a very strong candidate for membership in the G-7 and the OECD. As an interim step, it might be possible to grant China observer status in these organizations, much like Russia currently enjoys in the G-7.

## Conclusion

Implementing a WTO accession strategy like that envisioned here would be an enormously complex diplomatic task. Keeping a united front among major WTO members in the accession negotiations would be challenging, particularly with China attempting to disrupt the unified position using all of its considerable influence.

Negotiating with China would, of course, be equally challenging. It would need to be alternately threatened and cajoled into negotiating a sweeping series of reforms. It would certainly enjoy the benefits of WTO membership, but would try to maintain as much of its present mercantilistic system as possible. It is even possible that when the true scope of the necessary reforms became clear to China, it would prefer to put off WTO membership. In this case, the rest of the world would continue to employ interim measures, such as trade laws and bilateral negotiations, until China was prepared to move forward on the WTO. When all these factors are considered, a long and painful negotiation seems inevitable, unless the world simply accepts China's membership on China's terms.

This strategy, however, does have the virtue of being the only one that allows WTO members and, ultimately, China to "have their cake and eat it too." China is brought into the system and the system is actually strengthened instead of being weakened by a plethora of special breaks for China. The stage would be set for mutual growth of China and the world, and many of the seeds of economic conflict will have been removed. That is a goal truly worth working for.

## Notes

1. Joe Studwell, "EU, U.S. Split on China's WTO Bid," *Journal of Commerce,* November 18, 1996.

2. David Sanger, "U.S. to Spur Beijing on Trade Group Entry," *New York Times,* November 13, 1996.

3. Francesco Lao Xi Sisci, "Euro Chief Breathes New Life in China's WTO Bid," *Asia Times,* November 15, 1996.

4. Hijiri Inose, "Hashimoto Sets Japan's Agenda for This Week's G-7 Summit," *Nikkei Weekly,* June 24, 1996.

5. John Zarcostas, "West Upbeat on Taiwan Talks, Doubtful on China Progress," *Journal of Commerce,* July 26, 1993.

6. Some interesting stories on this topic can be found in Matt Forney, "Trial by Fire," *Far East Economic Review,* September 12, 1996.

7. Leah A. Haus, *Globalizing the GATT: The Soviet Union's Successor States, Eastern Europe, and the International Trading System* (Washington, DC: The Brookings Institution, 1992), 25–68.

8. Contracting Parties to the General Agreement on Tariffs and Trade, *Basic Instruments and Selected Documents,* 15th Supplement (Geneva: GATT, 1968).

9. Ibid.

10. Haus, *Globalizing the GATT,* 29.

11. For details of accession arrangements see Contracting Parties to the General Agreement on Tariffs and Trade, *Basic Instruments and Selected Documents,* 15th Supplement, 18th Supplement, and 20th Supplement, 1968, 1972, and 1974.

12. Ibid., 15th Supplement and 18th Supplement, 1968 and 1972.

13. Ibid.

14. Ibid., and M.M. Kostecki, *East-West Trade and the GATT System* (New York: St. Martin's Press, 1979), 117.

15. The language establishing the general safeguard appears in all three of the above-cited accession protocols, but was never triggered.

16. An excellent discussion can be found in Kostecki, *East-West Trade and the GATT System,* 91–133.

17. Ibid., 117.

18. Ibid.

19. Contracting Parties to the General Agreement on Tariffs and Trade, *Basic Instruments and Selected Documents,* 15th Supplement.

20. "U.S. Offers 'Road Map' to China's Entry into WTO," *Asian Economic News,* November 13, 1995; and "A Great Leap Forward," *Economist,* November 25, 1996.

21. "China's Road to the WTO," *EIU Business Asia,* May 20, 1996; and "EU Official Urges USA to Follow Europe on WTO Membership for China," *BBC Summary of World Broadcasts,* November 19, 1996.

22. "China Asks WTO to Keep Politics out of Membership Issue," *Agence France Presse,* April 25, 1996.

23. Lionel Barber, "China Pushes to Join GATT in EC Talks," *Financial Times,* April 29, 1993.

24. Greg Mastel, *China and the WTO: Economy at the Crossroad* (Washington, DC: Economic Strategy Institute, 1994), 32–36.

25. Greg Mastel, "A New U.S. Trade Policy Toward China," *Washington Quarterly* (winter 1996), 189–207.

26. Paul Blustein, "U.S. Urges China to Consider Import Targets to Open Economy," *Washington Post,* January 24, 1996.

27. Greg Mastel and Gregory Stanko, "Cheating on a Critical Alliance?" *Journal of Commerce,* December 5, 1995.

28. Jim Hoagland, "Trade with China Divides the Atlantic Alliance," *International Herald Tribune,* May 4, 1996.

29. Joe Studwell, "EU, U.S. Split on China's WTO Bid," *Journal of Commerce,* November 18, 1996.

30. Hijiri, "Hashimoto Sets Japan's Agenda for This Week's G-7 Summit."

31. Japan joined the GATT in 1955; Mexico joined in 1986.

32. Clyde Prestowitz, "China and the WTO: Not So Fast," *Journal of Commerce,* September 21, 1994.

33. *Review of the Uruguay Round, Commitments to Open Foreign Markets,* Hearings Before the Committee on Finance, United States Senate, April 18, 1991.

34. For a good brief discussion, see Leslie Helm, "In the Chips," *Los Angeles Times,* March 5, 1995.

35. Douglas A. Irwin, *Managed Trade: The Case Against Import Targets* (Washington, DC: American Enterprise Institute, 1994).

36. Contracting Parties to the General Agreement on Tariffs and Trade, *Final Texts of the GATT Uruguay Round Agreements Including the Agreement Establishing the World Trade Organization,* Agreement on Agriculture, Annex 5, Section A.2, April 15, 1994.

# Afterword: A New Era of China Diplomacy

In the modern era, relations between the western world and China have always had an air of excitement and urgency. When Nixon went to China, it was seen as the breakthrough that could bring China into the world and keep the Soviet Union at bay. After difficult and, in relative terms, extremely rapid diplomacy, enormous differences were bridged and the United States was able to play the "China card." Despite some setbacks, this chapter in U.S. diplomacy nearly lived up to its billing.[1]

In spite of the tragedy of Tiananmen Square and countless smaller setbacks, that air of excitement still seems to permeate western and particularly U.S. relations with China. Is it any wonder that today's generation of diplomats long for new triumphs with the Middle Kingdom, and that many see themselves as modern Henry Kissingers, forging ties between East and West?

No, it is not surprising in the least, but it is dangerous.

Today's key issues with China are economic, not diplomatic or military. The negotiation should be over tariffs and industrial policy, not nuclear weapons or containing the Russian bear. The discussion is really about the slow and often painful task of pulling an economy out of decades of communist economic dogma, not reining in a communist military power.

Still, the world seems to long for the old days. Diplomats often prefer to discuss more familiar but increasingly less relevant issues, like arms sales or nuclear reactor sales, and not economic and trade minutiae. Leaders often still seem inclined to make Cold War–era trade-offs on trade and economic concerns to achieve "progress" on one of these other more exciting issues.

Unfortunately, this kind of diplomacy is sorely out of date, irresponsible, and downright dangerous. The primary challenge now posed by China is an economic one. It is the handling of the economic minutiae that will, in large part, determine the future standard of living of Chinese citizens and the citizens of China's trading partners, as well as the health of the world economy. The time for playing the "China card" and diplomatic showboating is long past, and those who persist in it are doing the entire world a grave disservice. It is time to forget the high drama of the Cold War and get on with the serious business of building a world economy in which all, including China, can prosper, and all, including China, bear their share of the responsibility. This is the only way to truly advance the interests of China and the world.

## Note

1. Henry Kissinger, *The White House Years* (Boston: Little, Brown, 1979).

# Select Bibliography

Barton, John H., and Bart S. Fisher. *International Trade and Investment: Selected Documents.* New York: Little, Brown, 1986.

Bertsch, Gary K., and Richard T. Cupitt. "Nonproliferation in the 1990s: Enhancing International Cooperation on Export Controls." *Washington Quarterly* (fall 1993), 53–70.

Cai Wenguo. "China's GATT Membership: Selected Legal and Political Issues." *Journal of World Trade,* February 1992.

Calder, Kent. "Asia's Empty Gas Tank." *Foreign Affairs,* March/April 1996.

Central Intelligence Agency. *The World Factbook 1994.* Washington, DC: CIA Publications, 1994.

———. *The World Factbook 1995.* Washington, DC: CIA Publications, 1995.

———. *The World Factbook 1996.* Washington, DC: CIA Publications, 1996.

Chanda, Nayan. "The End Is Near." *Far Eastern Economic Review,* February 23, 1995, 48.

Ching, Frank, ed. *China in Transition.* Hong Kong: Far Eastern Economic Review Publication, 1994.

Cohen, Jerome A., and John E. Lange. "The Chinese Legal System—A Primer for Investors." *Investment Opportunities in China.* New York: Morgan Stanley, January 1995.

Collins, Susan M., and Barry P. Bosworth. *The New GATT: Implications for the United States.* Washington, DC: The Brookings Institution, 1994.

Contracting Parties to the General Agreement on Tariffs and Trade. *Basic Instruments and Selected Documents.* 15th Supplement. Geneva: GATT, 1968.

———. *Basic Instruments and Selected Documents.* 18th Supplement. Geneva: GATT, 1972.

———. *Basic Instruments and Selected Documents.* 20th Supplement. Geneva: GATT, 1974.

———. *Final Texts of the GATT Uruguay Round Agreement Including the Agreement Establishing to World Trade Organization.* April 15, 1994.

Finger, Michael J., and Andrzej Olechowski, eds. *The Uruguay Round: A Handbook for the Multilateral Trade Negotiations.* Washington, DC: The World Bank, 1987.

Forney, Matt. "Trial by Fire." *Far Eastern Economic Review,* September 12, 1996.

Harding, Harry. *A Fragile Relationship: The United States and China since 1972.* Washington, DC: The Brookings Institution, 1992.

Haus, Leah A. *Globalizing the GATT: The Soviet Union's Successor States, Eastern Europe, and the International Trading System.* Washington, DC: The Brookings Institution, 1992.

Herzstein, Robert E. "China and the GATT: Legal and Policy Issues Raised by China's Participation in the General Agreement on Tariffs and Trade." *Law and Policy in International Business,* 1986.

International Monetary Fund, *International Financial Statistics Yearbook, 1994.* Washington, DC: IMF, 1994.

———. *International Financial Statistics Yearbook, 1995.* Washington, DC: IMF, 1995.

———. *International Financial Statistics Yearbook, 1996.* Washington, DC: IMF, 1996.

Jackson, John. *The World Trading System.* Cambridge, MA: MIT Press, 1994.

Jacobson, Harold K., and Michel Oksenberg. *China's Participation in the IMF, the World Bank and the GATT: Toward a Global Economic Order.* (Ann Arbor: University of Michigan Press, 1990.)

Johnson, Bryan T., and Thomas P. Sheehy. *1996 Index of Economic Freedom.* Washington, DC: The Heritage Foundation, 1996.

Johnson, Chalmers. *Japan: Who Governs?* New York: W.W. Norton, 1995.

Kemme, David M. "Introduction: Technology Controls and Prospects for Change in the 1990s." In D. Kemme, ed., *Technology Markets and Export Controls in the 1990s.* New York: New York University Press, 1991.

Khan, Azizur Rahman, Keith Griffin, Carl Riskin, and Zhao Renwei. "Household Income and Its Distribution in China." *China Quarterly,* December 1992.

Kim, Kihwan, and Danny M. Leipziger. *The Lessons of East Asia. Korea: A Case of Government-Led Development.* Washington, DC: The World Bank, 1993.

Kirshner, Orin, ed. *The Bretton Woods-GATT System.* Armonk, NY: M.E. Sharpe, 1996.

Kohli, Sheel. "Mainland Gets Foot in WTO." *South China Morning Post,* July 25, 1995.

Kostecki, M.M. *East-West Trade and the GATT System.* New York: St. Martin's Press, 1979.

Kravis, Irving B. "An Approximation of the Relative Real Per Capita GDP of the People's Republic of China." *Journal of Comparative Economics,* March 1981.

Lardy, Nicholas R. "Chinese Foreign Trade." *China Quarterly,* September 1992.

———. *Foreign Trade and Economic Reform in China, 1978–1990.* Cambridge: Cambridge University Press, 1992.

Lubman, Stanley. "The Future of Chinese Law." *China Quarterly,* March 1995.

Ma Guonan, and Ross Garnaut. *How Rich Is China: Evidence from the Food Economy.* Working Papers in Trade and Development No. 92/4. Canberra: The Australian National University, Research School of Pacific Studies, 1992.

Mastel, Greg. *China and the WTO: Economy at the Crossroad.* Washington, DC: Economic Strategy Institute, 1994.

———. "The Art of the Steal." *Washington Post,* February 19, 1995.

———. "A New U.S. Trade Policy Toward China." *Washington Quarterly* (winter 1996).

———. "Trail of Broken Trade Vows." *Washington Times,* January 2, 1996.

———. "Piracy in China: No Mickey Mouse Issue." *Washington Post,* February 15, 1996.

———. "Living with the Chinese Dragon." *Journal of Commerce,* March 21, 1996.

———. *American Trade Laws after the Uruguay Round.* Armonk, NY: M.E. Sharpe, 1996.

———. "Beijing at Bay." *Foreign Policy* (fall 1996).

———. "Sober Look at China Investment." *Journal of Commerce,* October 18, 1996.

———. "China: Earning WTO Admission." *Journal of Commerce,* November 19, 1996.

Mastel, Greg, and Andrew Szamosszegi. "America's New Trade Nemesis," *International Economy,* May/June 1996.

*Memorandum of Understanding Between the Government of the People's Republic of China and the Government of the United States on the Protection of Intellectual Property,* 1992.

*Memorandum of Understanding Between the Government of the United States of America and the Government of the People's Republic of China Concerning Market Access,* 1992.

Minami, Ryoshin. *The Economic Development of China: A Comparison with the Japanese Experience.* New York: St. Martin's Press, 1994.

Morse, Ronald A. "Broken China?" *International Economy,* January/February 1995.

Palmeter, N. David. "The Impact of the U.S. Antidumping Law on China-U.S. Trade." *Journal of World Trade,* August 1991.

Parson, Margaret M. *Joint Ventures in the People's Republic of China: The Control of Foreign Direct Investment Under Socialism.* Princeton, NJ: Princeton University Press, 1991.

Pisani, Elizabeth. "EU Comes Courting with Vows of Support." *Asia Times,* November 14, 1996.

Prestowitz, Clyde V., Jr. *Trading Places.* New York: Basic Books, 1988.

———. "China and WTO: Not so Fast." *Journal of Commerce,* September 21, 1994.

Rohwer, Jim. "The Titan Stirs," *Economist,* November 28, 1992.

Sanger, David E. "U.S. to Spur Beijing on Trade Group Entry," *New York Times,* November 13, 1996.

Schott, Jeffrey J. *The Uruguay Round: An Assessment.* Washington, DC: The Institute for International Economics, November, 1994.

Shinn, James, ed. *Weaving the Net: Conditional Engagement with China.* New York: Council on Foreign Relations Press, 1996.

Shirk, Susan. *The Political Logic of Economic Reform in China.* Berkeley: University of California Press, 1993.

Spence, Jonathan D. *The Search for Modern China.* New York: W.W. Norton, 1990.

Sung Yun-wing. *The China-Hong Kong Connection: The Key to China's Open-Door Policy.* Cambridge: Cambridge University Press, 1991.

Swaine, Michael D. *China–Domestic Change and Foreign Policy.* Santa Monica, CA: RAND, 1995.

Taylor, Jeffrey. *Dollar GNP Estimates for China.* Center for International Research Staff Paper No. 59. Washington, DC: United States Bureau of the Census, March 1991.

Tyler, Patrick E. "Western Lift for China's Aircraft Plans." *New York Times,* February 25, 1995.

Tyson, Laura D'Andrea. *Who's Bashing Whom? Trade Conflict in High Technology Industries.* Washington, DC: Institute for International Economics, 1993.

United States Trade Representative. *1994 National Trade Estimate Report on Foreign Trade Barriers.* Washington, DC: USTR, 1994.

———. *1995 National Trade Estimate Report on Foreign Trade Barriers.* Washington, DC: USTR, 1995.

———. *1996 National Trade Estimate Report on Foreign Trade Barriers.* Washington, DC: USTR, 1996.

United States General Accounting Office. *Export Controls: Advising U.S. Business of Policy Changes.* Washington, DC: GAO, 1990.

United States International Trade Commission. *Annual Report 1993.* Washington, DC: ITC, 1993.

———. *Annual Report 1994.* Washington, DC: ITC, 1994.

———. *Operation of Trade Agreement Programs, 1985–1993.* Washington, DC: ITC, 1995.

van Brabant, Jozef M. *The Planned Economies and International Economic Organization.* Cambridge: Cambridge University Press, 1991.

Vines, Stephen. "Foreign Direct Investment in China Slows Down." *Business Times* (Singapore), January 23, 1995.

Vogel, Ezra. *One Step Ahead in China: Guangdong under Reform.* Cambridge, MA: Harvard University Press, 1989.

Wilhelm, Alfred D., Jr. *The Chinese at the Negotiating Table.* Washington, DC: National Defense University Press, February 1994.

World Bank. *China: Reform and the Plan in the 1990s.* Washington, DC: The World Bank, 1992.

———. *China Foreign Trade Reform.* Washington, DC: The World Bank, 1993.

———. *China Updating Economic Memorandum: Managing Rapid Growth and Transition.* Washington, DC: The World Bank, 1993.

————. *China: Foreign Trade Reform.* Washington, DC: The World Bank, 1994.

Ya Qin. "China and GATT: Accession Instead of Resumption." *Journal of World Trade* 27 (April) 1993.

Yu, Peter Kien-hong. "Federal System May Ease Coming Mainland Change." *Free China Journal.* November 25, 1994.

Zweig, David. "Developmental Communities on China's Coast: The Impact of Trade, Investment, and Transnational Alliance." *Comparative Politics.* April 1995.

# Index

Greg Mastel is vice president for policy planning and administration at the Economic Strategy Institute (ESI). He joined ESI in October 1994. Dr. Mastel is also an adjunct professor at the University of Maryland UC Graduate School of Management and Technology. Previously, he worked in the U.S. Senate for eight years in various posts, including chief international trade adviser to the chairman of the Senate Finance Committee's International Trade Subcommittee. While working in the Senate, Dr. Mastel was an official congressional adviser to U.S. trade negotiators and worked on issues including extension of fast-track trade negotiating authority, the Uruguay Round trade agreement, MFN status for China, Super 301, and the North American Free Trade Agreement.

Dr. Mastel holds a Ph.D. in International Economics and an MBA. He is a member of a number of economic and trade advisory boards. Dr. Mastel frequently writes and provides analysis for the *Washington Post*, the *Los Angeles Times*, the *Washington Times*, the *Wall Street Journal*, and many other publications. He also writes a regular column on economics and trade for the *Journal of Commerce* and has appeared on CNN, NBC, ABC, and the "Nightly Business Report." Dr. Mastel is the author of *American Trade Laws after the Uruguay Round* (1996).